CU00797456

Towards Little Germany

Norman Ellis

Published by Low Moor Local History Group, Bradford
c/o 13, St Abbs Fold, Odsal, Bradford BD6 1EL ☎ 01274 673274

Acknowledgements

In addition to the acknowledgements which appear in the text of the book, I must express my sincere appreciation to the contribution made by Geoff and Mary Twentyman, without whose unstinting help, our goal would not have been achieved.

I am also greatly indebted to Eric Slicer for the photographs and for the time spent with me looking at the buildings of Little Germany.

Many thanks to Joan Waddington for reading the script and the map for the trail.

I must also express my thanks to the staff of the Reference Library, and in particular to Mr R. J. Duckett, whose advice and practical help to a complete novice were absolutely invaluable, though I have to say with regret, that in the end the Library was unable to proceed with the project, due, I was informed, to cuts in the Council's budget.

First published 1997
Text: Copyright © Norman Ellis 1997
Map: Copyright © Joan Waddington 1997
Photographs: for Copyright see page 82
Printed by: Indent Services (Leeds) Co., Pudsey.

ISBN 0 9527427 1 3

By the same author "Low Moor, the beginning of a journey"
Published by the Low Moor Local History Group - 1996

Contents

Part One - Working Days

Part Two - Back To The Beginning

For Harriet

My Granddaughter

Towards Little Germany

Introduction

A few years ago, possibly as long ago as 1981, I sat down with a notebook and a pencil and, just as a quiet mental exercise, began to write down as many names as I could remember of the people who were employed by Law, Russell & Co. Ltd. at 63 Vicar Lane, Bradford, when I worked there more than sixty years ago, during the period 1927 to 1930.

In the first instance I had not the slightest intention of arranging my memories in the form of a book, but I was amazed to discover that I was able to remember the names of no fewer than eighty employees, nearly all male, and in a wide age range of between fifteen and sixty-five and possibly older.

It was a year or two later, perhaps, that my mind turned once again to those years at Law, Russell's, no doubt as a result of the public concern being expressed regarding the urgent need to save for posterity, as well as for today's citizens of the city, the fine old buildings, notably Paper Hall and the warehouses of Little Germany.

My interest being re-kindled by all the publicity, I began to jot down a few of my memories of working in the area, just as they came to me, still with no other thought than that of testing out my ability to recall incidents and to record my impressions of former days. When I applied myself to the task of making a few notes about my experiences, one thing became very clear; in spite of the urge to record as much as I could remember of my life in an office in Little Germany during the years of 1927 - 1930, memories which I found gave me a great deal of satisfaction to recall, I did find it rather difficult to divorce information concerned with my life in Little Germany, from my life and experiences away from the office, this meant that I was quite unable to keep Low Moor, my home district, out of the story! I was determined however, that it should be principally the story of my early business life in Little Germany, within the setting of the times, which were the years of the late 1920s.

It would be impossible, I think, for me to give a straightforward reason for my decision to write a little book, however incompetently, as so many influences had brought me to the point of decision, chief among which was the fact that I had recently purchased a small computer with word-processing facilities, and this was crying out for exercise!

Having taken the decision to set down my recollections, I had to learn fairly quickly how to do certain things. Firstly, how to operate the computer so that it really was quicker than using a typewriter, and secondly, how to put my thoughts in order ready for typing. Even at the age of eighty-two, although I found it all more than a little difficult to begin with, (and to be honest, I still do!) I discovered as one usually does, that with perseverance I was able to control the sometimes wild activities of the computer, as well as my own mental meanderings, and in due course I managed to produce some fairly readable material; but the reader must be the final arbiter in this regard

Towards Little Germany

PART ONE

WORKING DAYS

(My memories of Little Germany)

CHAPTER ONE

I Start My First Job

The year 1926 was a memorable one! It was the year of the General Strike, and it was also the year that I left Grange Road Secondary School, Bradford, and began the search for a job. Jobs were scarce and becoming more so. I had no real idea of what I wanted to do, but I had a vague notion that I would like to work in an office, in spite of the fact that several of my father's friends advised him against encouraging this idea. However, I registered with the Juvenile Employment Bureau in Manor Row, put my name down for a Commercial Course at Carlton Street Evening School, kept an eye on the "Situations Vacant" column in the "Telegraph" (we were a "Telegraph" as opposed to an "Argus" family) and waited.

It was during this period that I was introduced by a school friend to Mr. Sam Woodhead, a Director of The Bradford Dyers' Association, who was keenly interested in the welfare of boys, and ready to advise and offer practical help in many ways. For example, should one of the boys who came within his sphere of influence be in need of medical or surgical treatment, then Mr. Woodhead would arrange that the boy received the best possible advice and treatment.

Although at this time he was himself suffering from a heart condition, he liked his boys to drop in occasionally for a chat in his office at 39, Well Street. I recall that whenever I called to see him he used to greet me with a kiss, which, even for a sixteen-year-old was not unpleasant, as he was always so clean and fresh-looking with a delicately perfumed waxed moustache.

He loved to talk about his son Sir John Woodhead whose photograph (or was it a painting) hung on the wall of Mr. Woodhead's office showing Sir John in court dress, with knee breeches, sword and sash. I believe he was a member of the Indian Diplomatic Service, but I'm not very sure about this and I may have been mistaken. In any case it was obviously a position of some note.

Mr. Woodhead was very fond of peaches and I recall that on more than one occasion he sent me up to the Home and Colonial Fruit Stores in Rawson Place for three peaches, one of which, of course, he gave to me. I remember also that soon after I met him he sent me along to a photographer's named Gunston & Co., whose studio was in Manningham Lane, just beyond the top of Cheapside. Presumably he wanted a copy of my photograph to keep in his records. I still have a copy . Did I really look so young and handsome in those days?

It was Mr. Woodhead's wish that none of his boys should marry before the age of twenty-five, but to a boy of sixteen this restriction posed no problems at all. He gave me a card, similar to a folding club card or syllabus; I can't remember if it had a title but I do remember that it set out his "Rules for Good Living", which advice included, the words of Adam in Shakespeare's "As You Like It" :-

> "Though I look old, yet am I strong and lusty,
> For in my youth I never did apply
> Hot and rebellious liquors in my blood
> Nor did not with unbashful forehead
> Woo the means of weakness and debility"

Eventually, after some weeks I was given a card at the Juvenile Employment Bureau to go for an interview at the firm of Law, Russell & Co., Ltd., in Vicar Lane. Of course I had never heard of such a company, but my father, who worked for the Bradford Dyers' Association in either East Parade or Harris Street at that time, knew them to be an old-established and well-respected firm in Bradford textile circles. I decided that no harm would be done if I called to let Mr. Woodhead know of my good fortune. He quickly had his secretary, whose name I believe was Marion, type out a letter of introduction to the management of Law, Russell's. Full of the confidence of youth, and armed with Mr. Woodhead's letter, I went along to be interviewed by Mr. Leach, the Counting House Manager. I can remember nothing of the interview, except for two of the questions I was asked :- "Do you know anyone who works here?" and "Do you go to Sunday School?". Since I, my father and my grandfather had all been associated with Church and Sunday School activities for as long as I could remember, the answer was most definitely in the affirmative! I had learned from my father, just prior to the interview, that he knew a Low Moor lad who worked for Law, Russell's whose name was Wilfred Garnett; he was a few years older than me, but I knew him quite well. I must have given satisfactory answers to the remainder of the questions for I started work in the Counting House as Office Boy, at a wage of 12/6d per week. This would be early in 1927.

I did call to see Mr. Woodhead on one or two occasions. It was only a few minutes walk from Vicar Lane to his office and I remember a particular time when I called to see him. I had knocked on his office door, and although I didn't on this occasion hear his "Come in", I opened the door slightly, just to make sure whether he was in or out of the office. Unfortunately, he was in but apparently just experiencing a severe heart attack. His secretary, Marion, was in attendance and when I offered to go in she motioned for me to leave, which I did immediately. I never saw him again.

CHAPTER TWO

The Bell And The Smell

Mr. Leach was the best of bosses. I soon had the same respect for him that the boys of Rugby School were reputed to have had for Dr. Arnold. He was a very quiet, efficient gentleman of almost Edwardian appearance. His back was very straight, whether walking or sitting, due, I used to think, to the sort of collars he wore, the very deep, stiff white collars that had ceased to be fashionable even in those days! I never saw him angry and never heard him raise his voice above normal. He was a perfect gentleman. I never lost my regard for him and I shall always remember him with real affection.

It was a great pleasure for me, a few years later, to find myself singing in the same "augmented" choir on at least two occasions. After Law, Russell's ceased trading, I believe he went to work at the Bradford Royal Infirmary as a secretary, before becoming Secretary of the Craig Convalescent Home, from which position I think he went into retirement.

Right from the start I felt that the building at 63, Vicar Lane, was rather special and one of the most impressive warehouse buildings that I had ever seen. I still do! In the course of the last fifty years or so, I have made it a practice of popping up to Vicar Lane, just to see how "The Old Lady" was getting along; after all, she was born in 1874.

I am indebted to the excellent little booklet by Mr. John S. Roberts entitled "Little Germany" for giving me so much pleasure by reminding me of the many splendid buildings that I knew so well in the late 20s, and which were occupied by such well-respected firms as Priestley's, Kessler's, Firth & Marshall, Downs, Coulter and, of course A & S Henry in Leeds Road which I passed several times a day, as I did the imposing building occupied by the Bradford Dyers' Association Ltd., in Well Street.

But for me, there was, and is, no other building in Bradford to match the Law, Russell building, with its imposing front entrance and its two pairs of Corinthian pillars, above which, on each floor are similar impressive pillars at either side of the corner windows. The 5-tier portico being surmounted by a huge canopy with an iron cresting which always looked to me like a crown! I still look at it with admiration occasionally as I pass through the Interchange.

In order to reach the ground floor offices from the front entrance it was necessary to climb five or six steps on the left, and inside the entrance hall was the lift shaft, encircled by a magnificent staircase and balustrade. On the right was the office in which the telephone switchboard was located. Miss Hodgson was the switch-board operator and the lift attendant was Sergeant James Redman. I think that in his spare time "Jim" was a bookies' runner within the firm; either that or he did an awful lot of betting on his own account! I know that whenever I was the relief switch-board operator at lunch time, Jim would usually pick up the telephone in one of the vacant offices upstairs and ask "Will you put me through, Norman?" which meant that he wanted to be put through to the exchange so that he could ask for the number himself. We soon got wise to this ruse, of course.

At the commencement of my employment with Law, Russell's there was one thing that I was quite certain about and that was that I would never, ever get used to the SMELL! Whatever could it be? It was rather like the smell of cheese, Gorgonzola cheese, long past its "Sell by" date. But it couldn't be - could it? I seemed to notice this peculiar aroma more especially at lunch time, and for a few days it was almost more than my stomach could stand!

As we had no canteen facilities for the Counting House staff, the juniors used to take a "mashing" of tea in a pint pot, through the Grey Room, across the Delivery Yard and down the steps to the Boiler Room, where Barak Day (see Judges Chapter 4 verse 6), the really diminutive boiler man who wore corduroy trousers, a denim jacket and a cloth cap, kept a geyser of water on the boil for tea making. We then took our pots of tea into the Grey Room and, taking out our sandwiches or whatever, we proceeded to sit on the grey pieces and eat in comfort, or would have done so but for the SMELL!

Until I got used to it, it nearly did make me physically sick! Fortunately it didn't take very long for me to master my objections once I had discovered the origin of the problem. It wasn't the smell of the grey pieces; in fact, it wasn't the smell of pieces at all, but the smell of blankets - NEW WOOL blankets! UGGH!

The basement of the building at 63 Vicar Lane, as well as accommodating the Boiler Room, Coal Storage and General Repository for old company records, worn-out typewriters, bits of machinery and so on, was also, and more importantly, the Blanket Room. Here, the Manager, Mr. Bradbury, his deputy Fred Collett and, I think, one other warehouseman whose name I have forgotten (if I ever knew it), controlled the storage and despatch of hundreds of pairs of wool blankets, most of them probably woven in the mills of Wormalds & Walker at Dewsbury.

I recall that when I became accustomed to visiting the department in connection with my normal duties, I was interested to see the blankets being brushed with large "teasel" brushes, which operation was carried out, I suppose, to get rid of the fluff before the blankets were despatched to customers. I remember using some of this waste material to make a nice comfortable bed for my white mice!

In the late 1920's the finest Yorkshire All-wool Blankets - "Super Lawrus" we called them - sold for I think, One Hundred Shillings (£5) per pair! Unless my memory is at fault, Fred Collett hailed from Little Horton and he was either organist or deputy organist at St. Oswald's Church.

Straight ahead from the top of the entrance steps was the door leading into the Counting House and immediately inside the door was the "ENQUIRIES" window; beyond again, and a little to the left was the Office Desk, from which the office-boys operated.

Stanley was in charge when I arrived on the scene and I liked him from the beginning. His name was Stanley Robertshaw and his home was in East Bowling. His father also worked for Law, Russell's in the Top Room, I believe. When I started it meant that Stanley received a little promotion, and for a few weeks everything I did I had learnt from Stanley. I am sure that he quite enjoyed being the senior office boy. He was probably about seventeen years of age at the time, while I was only sixteen! We got on splendidly together and I don't remember a single dispute between us at any time. He, of course, was eager to show me all the duties that had to be carried out, and I was more than willing to learn; it was an exciting but important time, and I enjoyed it immensely!

I would have done anything within reason for Stanley. There always seemed to be such a lot of work waiting to be done, but somehow we found time for a bit of fun as well - "larking about" the old ledger clerks would have called it if they had known of some of our escapades. I don't remember that we did anything very reprehensible, unless it was the taking of the odd cigarette from the box on the table in Mr. James's office - Rothman's I believe they were! I don't know who smoked them, apart from the office boys now and again, because most of the Directors were pipe smokers, as were all the senior clerks with one or two exceptions, notably Raymond Veal the assistant Cashier, who smoked cigarettes. No doubt they were simply for the use of visitors!

I soon learned that one of my most important duties was "ANSWERING THE BELL!" On the wall, near to the office desk was "THE BELL" and beneath it were the indicator flags in the familiar glass-fronted box. When the bell was rung, the movement of one of the flags would indicate whether we were summoned to the large

14

Board Room, occupied by Mr. James D. Law, to the smaller office adjoining it which was occupied by Mr. Kenneth W. Law, or to the "ENQUIRIES" window. So, if one of us left the desk unattended, to take a message, go to the Post Office, or simply to mind our own business, it was usual for us to cry out "ANSWER THE BELL, PLEASE" before disappearing in the direction of the "Grey Room" which was next door.

Mr. J.D. Law, or Mr. James as he was known by all throughout the firm was, I think, the eldest of three brothers, all directors of the company, the others being Mr. Kenneth and Mr. Ralph. These gentlemen being two of the four members of staff who, unfortunately each had an artificial leg, due to wounds received in the First World War; the others being Willie Catling and one of the Magson brothers, Herbert, I think,

Mr. James was the Belgian Consul in Bradford, but he made few demands upon the services of the office boys. It took me a little time to get used to what I thought must be a cultured accent, although at first I simply thought that he was a chronic catarrh sufferer. He did however, ring for us now and then to "Pop along to Moffat & Saunders" in Market Street for his favourite tobacco - "Bank Mixture" which, came in a lavender blue packet; or to "Slip across to Lupton's" in Cheapside, generally for a previously ordered bottle of whisky.

I believe that Mr. Kenneth was the Company Secretary and I distinctly remember that his choice of weed was "IMPI", available from most tobacconists. Mr. Ralph's office was on the third floor I think, so perhaps he didn't choose to call upon us very often, but I do remember that his favourite tobacco was "AFRICANDER". Whenever any of these gentlemen passed through the Counting House, they invariably trailed behind them a dense cloud of blue smoke that never completely dispersed since it was always being added to by the members of the senior clerical staff. For almost to a man they smoked furiously all day long!

Next to Mr. Kenneth's office was that of the Cashier, Mr. Sugden and his assistant Raymond Veal. I think Mr. Sugden lived in the Eccleshill area, while Raymond Veal I am quite sure lived in rooms in White's View, Whetley Hill. The Cashier's Office was really one long mahogany desk, partitioned off from the rest of the Counting House. Next again was the double-sided desk at which the ledger clerks stood, or sat on high stools like so many Bob Cratchits! Their names were Bottomley London, Fred Pawson, Ralph Hall and a young woman named Lina Walker. I think I have got this last name correct as I had never heard the name "Lina" before.

After I had been working at Law, Russell's for some time, I don't remember exactly how long, but Mr. Sugden's son Norman came to join the ledger clerks. I used to think that, the three male clerks already named must have been at least seventy years of age, but now, on reflection, I think they were probably no more than fifty-five or sixty, but they looked like old men to us lads!

Lina Walker was the wife of Herbert Walker, the firm's maintenance man, and Norman Sugden came to replace her when she left to have a baby. If my recollection of events is correct, Lina Walker left the firm one day and had her baby the next, so she just made it! Norman Sugden I believe played cricket as a fast bowler with Eccleshill Cricket Club.

In a small office all to himself was Mr. Charles Dodgson, whose particular responsibility was "THE BANK"! I knew very little of what his job entailed except that it was concerned with Bills and Drafts and similar documents.

I recall that I was frequently required to go to the Inland Revenue Office at the top of Manor Row, in order to have some documents stamped.

Mr. Dodgson was a rather short man who walked with a kind of rolling gait, especially when he returned from an extended lunch, breathing whisky fumes on all and sundry, and just a little tipsy. I recall that it was not unusual for his wife to ring up the following morning to explain his non-appearance in the office by saying that he had had a "bad night"! Incidentally, Mr. Dodgson was another in that large band of heavy smokers who were employed at Law, Russell's.

CHAPTER THREE

Keeping Everyone Happy

As an introduction to the job of invoice typist the office boys were given responsibility for the House Sales Invoices, which meant that they were required to work out the calculations, type out the invoices and then distribute them to the respective members of staff. A few mistakes here and there on Home Sales Invoices didn't matter as much as when these things happened with customers' invoices. Nothing was considered to be worse than incorrect or badly typed invoices, so we had to learn the art by typing the House Sales Invoices to start with. After a few months we were ready to move on to full-scale invoicing duties. It was after this learning period that I had an experience of the kind that one doesn't easily forget.

A few of us were working late before going off to evening classes. I was sitting typing at a sloping desk, perhaps not a very wise thing to do, because at some point I leaned back, tilting the stool on which I was sitting, overbalanced and fell off the stool, bringing the typewriter with me which fell on the floor with a fearful crash, badly damaging the machine.

I had no alternative but to report the damage to Mr. Leach the following morning. When I assured him that the accident was due to carelessness and not the result of horse-play, he agreed to put the repair through, without reference to the directors. This was probably the first indication I had that things were becoming difficult for the firm, and that a certain amount of tightening-up was taking place!

In the course of the four years or so that I spent at Law, Russell's there was, of course, some movement of staff within the firm, so it should not be supposed that the junior clerks and typists named were doing the same job throughout their time at Law, Russell's or even that they remained in the same department. There was a steady progression from the office desk to the desks of the more senior clerks, so that when I arrived on the scene, the office desk was manned by Stanley and myself, then Stanley was promoted to fill a vacancy upstairs in the Entering Room. The vacancy left on the office desk was filled either by Ronald Dixon or by Harry Emmett, but I can't remember who came first. Further up the office were the more senior clerks, Willie Clarkson, who I believe, came from Burley-in-Wharfedale, Kenneth Ainsworth, Alan Gostick and Arnold Jagger.

17

One member of staff was an ardent racing fan, and to save any possible embarrassment I will call him "Seth" though that wasn't his name. I noticed that he seemed to spend quite a lot of time reading his newspaper, which was usually out of sight below his desk. He used to send me each morning for the "Sporting Pink", and just as frequently I was asked to go for the "Last City" edition of the "Telegraph"; it had to be a "Last City", nothing else would do, presumably because that was the only paper that would give him all the results of the day's racing! It was on the streets from four-thirty in the afternoon.

This business of being sent out for the racing papers went on for some months and I began to loathe the very idea, for it was contrary to all my upbringing. One day, however, it became clear that help was on the way. I had been up to Manor Row in the course of my legitimate duties - to get some documents stamped. On the way back I was caught in the most tremendous downpour. I remember thinking that I had never seen anything quite like it! I sheltered in an office doorway for a time, but it was no use, and there was a lot of mail awaiting my attention, so I just had to risk it.

When I did get back to the office I was completely soaked. As I went through the Counting House door who should be waiting for me but "Seth", with his usual request for me to fetch his "Last City". This was my big chance and mustering all my courage I refused to go!! When Mr. Leach saw the condition I was in he sent me straight home. I was never again sent out for a racing paper, and I don't know if anything passed between "Seth" and Mr. Leach, but it was a great relief to me and from that moment life took on an entirely new meaning!

The mail was an important part of the office-boys' responsibility. It had to be collected each morning from the Private Box section of the G.P.O. in Forster Square, and when I first started collecting it, the large leather mail-bag was almost more than I could manage, not only because of its size, but also because of its weight when it was so full that it could hardly be closed and locked. As I grew bigger and stronger, however, it ceased to be a problem. After the morning mail was collected, the bag was taken to Mr. James's office, where, around 8.15am Mr. Sugden would arrive to unlock the bag and sort the mail in time for the arrival of the directors, about nine o'clock. A second collection of mail was made later in the morning, for which a much smaller bag was used. The main interest shown by the various departments in this second bag of mail, was in the number of orders it contained which required immediate despatch. Normally such orders presented no problem; orders for material that was in stock would generally be entered, despatched and invoiced by six o'clock the same day. The problems arose on Saturday mornings - or would have done if the office-boys hadn't altered, ever so slightly, the course of events!

It was noticeable that nearly everyone who arrived for work on Saturday mornings found it difficult to give their minds completely to the job in hand. Most of the employees arrived dressed in readiness for the afternoon's leisure activities, e.g. sports coats and flannels, plus-fours, tennis shirts etc., and they couldn't get off the premises quickly enough! Consequently, should the office-boy arrive back from the G.P.O. with a bag full of orders in the second mail, he was likely to be distinctly unpopular. Where would you find a boy who courted unpopularity?

We devised therefore, a little scheme that was designed to keep everyone happy. Invoices and statements were, in those days, usually sent in unsealed envelopes, bearing a 1/2 d (half-penny) stamp, while orders were generally sent in sealed envelopes under a 1d. (one penny) stamp! So, on Saturday mornings when the large mail-bag was collected by the office-boy, and before taking the bag through to the private office, it was the work of a moment only, to slip one's hand under the flap of the locked bag, and extract a couple of handfuls of mail, and then to put back into the bag, all except perhaps a dozen or so UNSEALED envelopes which we knew did not contain orders, simply because they were unsealed 1/2 penny stamped envelopes! These unsealed envelopes were then placed in the small mail-bag, to be produced shortly after eleven o'clock as if the mail had just been collected from the Post Office! I wonder if any of the managers ever wondered why there were never any orders in the second mail on Saturday mornings? I don't suppose so, but we knew why!

After we had collected the morning mail, the next job was the distributing of the ledgers to the desks of the clerks from whom they had been collected the previous evening. One of the last duties of the day was the loading of the books and ledgers on to an iron trolley and then trundling them along to the strong-room, where they were locked up for the night. To push a trolley loaded to a height of four feet or so, was no mean feat for a small boy. It was at first rather like tackling an obstacle course. To get that heavy unwieldy iron monster into the strong-room without mishap was a major achievement.

First of all, it was pushed along the corridor past the private office, then a quick left turn was required, followed by a sharp right turn into the strong-room. It was necessary to develop a certain skill in order to execute this manoeuvre, which was made even more difficult because of the fact that across the front of the doorway of the strong-room was a brass strip which covered the edge of the linoleum. So, in order to perform the exercise correctly, one had to learn just when to give the trolley an extra push, and when to hang on to it to prevent its forward motion into the walk-way of the strong-room, without bringing it to a sudden stop.

Failure to carry out this procedure correctly meant that the load of ledgers would begin to rock ominously and, until one got the hang of it, simply fall backwards on to the floor with a tremendous crash, sometimes even damaging the ledgers, which were thong binders. Fortunately, as we also had to carry out this operation in reverse, of course, every morning, it wasn't long before this twice-daily exercise became child's play.

As well as being involved with the incoming mail, we were, obviously, also concerned with the large volume of out-going mail which was either collected by the office-boys from the various departments, or it was brought to the office desk to be weighed and stamped. A supply of stamps was always kept in the desk drawer, and no doubt this was considered to be reasonably secure as the stamps were perforated "L R & Co.". I suppose the occasional stamp was taken, but as far as I can remember, there was no widespread use of the firm's stamps on private letters. The bulk stocks were kept under lock and key by the assistant cashier, to whom we applied when we needed to replenish our own stocks.

I was intrigued in the early days to discover how many knives of a distinct type were used in the office. These were usually bone-handled knives with pear-shaped blades, and they were used by the ledger clerks. I don't know if they had a special name, but I do know that they were used for scratching out errors. They seemed to be continually in demand by one of the clerks, for use on ledgers, day books and receipt books, especially the latter in my case!

One of the tasks of the office-boy was to write out receipts for remittances received each day. In those days a Stamp Duty was imposed on all receipts of £2 and over. The receipt forms were bound in books, each page of which had perhaps four perforated receipt forms, each with its blue oval-shaped stamp already printed on it. The receipts looked almost as elaborate as did the company's cheques! When we had finished writing out the receipts, they had to be "called off", or checked against the statements with one of the ledger clerks, usually Fred Pawson. It was when we had to make alterations to a receipt that the "scratching out knife" was put to such good use!

I don't remember exactly when the momentous change took place, but eventually we were joined in the Counting House by two young ladies, namely Josephine Brady and Marie Crossley. They were employed as invoice and general typists at the Field Street end of the office, where Mr. Leach had his desk. At the opposite side of the office was the Elliot-Fisher machine. This was, to me, a most unusual machine indeed, since the other typewriters were mostly Remingtons or Underwoods. The Elliot-Fisher was a larger affair altogether, with a flat typing surface instead of a roller, and the typewriter itself could be moved over the flat surface up and down, back and forth, in fact it could be operated with a circular motion if required! This machine was used mainly for Export Invoices because of its powerful action and its ability to make a large number of copies.

Alan Gostick operated this machine for some time after my arrival at the firm, but eventually, due to promotions, this work became my responsibility. I can't remember what happened to Arnold Jagger; I think he must have left the firm because Alan Gostick was given his job as Petty Cashier and it was then that I was promoted and given the job (among others) of Export Invoice Typist and so became the operator of the notorious Elliot-Fisher!

CHAPTER FOUR

Trams And Tram Stoppers

One day, when I was still on the office desk, we were informed that a Mr. Shaw of Tapp and Toothill's would be coming along to demonstrate a Postal Franking Machine, and that he would stay with us until we had "done the mail". There were problems right from the start, chief of which was the fact that when the mail arrived on the desk to be posted, it came in all shapes and sizes, and any packets or envelopes which contained patterns, simply could not be put through the machine because they were too bulky. It became necessary, therefore, first to weigh the complete package and make a pencil note on the envelope of the value of the postage required, then to empty out the contents and put the empty envelope through the machine after which, the correct amount of postage was put on it, and finally everything was put back into the envelope.

This procedure saved no time at all, and with our sort of efficiency there was a grave risk that some of the contents would get into the wrong envelopes or even be dropped into the waste paper basket by mistake! I recall that we were very late getting away that first evening, and for a few evenings afterwards! Needless to say, we were not very pleased with the innovation, and it was clear that a solution would have to be found. Consequently, it wasn't very long before we were supplied with gummed slips which were printed with the company's name so that, when a bulky package had been weighed, a slip could easily be put through the machine, franked with the correct amount of postage and then stuck on the package. That, at least, was one problem solved, but there were others!

One of these problems revealed itself when it became necessary to re-ink the roller on the machine! The system was that when the impression made by the franking machine became somewhat faint, we were required to paint red ink on to the roller, as had been demonstrated by Mr. Shaw; but Mr. Shaw was a salesman/demonstrator, and as such, was something of an expert! Nobody mentioned that in the re-inking process we were likely to get red ink on our hands, on our faces and clothing, as well as all over the rest of the mail! I suppose that in the end we learned to make a reasonable job of it, as we did with most of our duties, but when I look at the perfect impressions that I see on mail that is delivered to my home nowadays, I have to admit that they give not the slightest hint of the agony that we went through in the early days of the Postal Franking Machine!

The Sales Day Books were collected each afternoon from the departments upstairs, chiefly from the Entering Department, where Percy Parker was in charge, and whose deputy was Eddie Peatfield. As soon as the daybooks were brought to the counting House it was the duty of the Clerks who were next in seniority after the office-boys, to "rule-off" individual items and highlight each customer's name in red ink. Once this was done, the next step was to carry out the calculations and total the amount of the invoice. For this purpose there were two calculating machines in use; one was a comptometer and the other a Burroughs calculating machine. I have a feeling that we had a Burroughs adding machine as well, but the Comptometer, as I recall, was a much heavier one to operate than the Burroughs, but for some reason it was preferred by most of us. I don't think that it took more than a month or two for us to become fairly proficient in carrying out the necessary calculations on these machines. Repeated use of the decimal fractions involved meant that we very soon learnt to keep these five-figure numbers in our heads, which speeded up the work quite significantly.

After this stage had been concluded and after the calculations had been checked, the books were then passed forward to the typists. Priority had always to be given to the entries which were marked "TONIGHT CERTAIN". The orders having been executed and the goods despatched generally by rail carrier, the aim now was to get the respective invoices away the same day that the goods were despatched, so that there should be no delay. The buyer needed to be able to check the consignment immediately, with regard to the length of the pieces, as well as being able to check that the material was exactly as ordered and according to the invoice.

A great deal of artificial silk material was dealt with in this manner, and I remember that large quantities of material with the name "CAMRUSYL" and with the Law, Russell number of 22579, was purchased by such firms as Ashley, Russell & Co. Ltd, and H.E. Closs & Co. Ltd., both firms having shops in many parts of the country, particularly in the south. I do recall, thought, that H.E. Closs's did have a shop in Bradford. It was in Kirkgate at the corner of Queensgate, in the premises now occupied by Millett's.

As I think about the urgency that was impressed upon us for dealing with the "TONIGHT CERTAIN" invoices, which were always sent under a 1d stamp, I recall with a little shame, an occasion when, because of a particularly large delivery of Ashley, Russell's shops, two or three of us were required to work one Saturday afternoon. Overtime payments for office staff were not even dreamt of in those days, though I believe some cash was made available to enable us to buy food. I think it was Alan Gostick and myself who went out shopping for our lunch requirements, and we just had to visit the Open-air Market, where there was a wonderful variety of attractions.

Anyone still living, who used to visit the Open-air Market in the 1920's and 30's, especially on a Saturday afternoon, will remember "MICKEY". With his loud voice and his pseudo-insulting manner he operated as a mock auctioneer or "cheap-jack" salesman. He was very popular and usually had a quite a large crowd gathered around him, not only on Saturday afternoons, but also, as I discovered later, on Thursdays too. That was the day when so many unemployed men had to "sign on", and after drawing their "dole money" they used to make their way up to the market for a little free entertainment. One could spend an hour there quite easily.

There was another "turn", a woman who did her act blindfolded who called herself Madam - something or other, I can't remember what - but I believe she was supposed to be a clairvoyant and she entertained the onlookers by giving details of various personal items in their possession, such as dates of coins, numbers on pound notes etc., of course with the expert help of an assistant! I don't think I ever discovered what she was able to persuade the gullible to part with their precious money for! There was also a man who sold penknives, the blades of which were "sharper than a mother-in-law's tongue", and these knives had a glass cutter which could cut glass as easily as butter, or so he said! This did appeal to me at the time, and I fell for it, and for some little time afterwards I would go around cutting pieces of broken glass into thin strips, but I'm sure this enthusiasm didn't last very long.

In due course we went back to the office with our purchases of bread and cheese and ate our lunch, after which we got on with the job in hand and finished typing out the invoices, then off we went to enjoy what was left of Saturday.

It was Monday morning when we got back to the office to find that the invoices which had caused all the extra work (and a little incidental entertainment) lay there on the office desk, all sealed, all with their 1d stamps affixed, - but unposted!! I don't remember that anything happened by way of complaint, and we certainly didn't admit to anyone what we had done, but we thought ourselves very lucky to get away with such carelessness. I'm quite sure that we never allowed the same mistake to occur again, ever!

In those days there was no official tea-break. However, this situation presented no problem to the junior office staff. Only a couple of streets away, at the junction of Park Gate and Peckover Street was a little house-shop, known to us as "Ma Rogan's ", and here, for a copper or two, we could purchase a pot of tea, and what was commonly known as a "Tram Stopper". The "Tram Stopper" was a large square block

24

of soggy confectionery about two and a half inches square and two inches thick, presumably made from all the buns and cakes left over in the bakery at the end of the day, to which had been added a quantity of fruit juice, to bind the whole lot together. In no other way could we account for the variety of colour and texture; but for growing lads with a large appetite this was the ideal mid-morning snack when accompanied by a half-pint of steaming hot tea!

I forget what others did, but at lunch-time I would sometimes slip around to the butcher's shop in Forster Square for a saveloy or for a couple of ounces of haslet to eat with three or four slices of buttered home-made bread. Quite often I would pay a visit, not only on my own account, but as errand boy for other members of the office staff, to the little confectioner's shop occupied by Mr. and Mrs. Duce, which was in Leeds Road, just above Chapel Street. This was a busy little shop, especially just before lunch-time (we always called it "dinner-time" in those days!) Philip Smith's pies were always popular and I often used to find that one or two were on my shopping list.

Frequently on Fridays for some reason that was not quite clear to me, I would be asked to fetch several lots of fish and chips from Peel Street Fisheries, which was always very busy on Fridays. It was there, I recall, that I first became aware of one of the facts of life, for hanging above the chip pan was a card bearing the injunction - "PLEASE DO NOT ASK FOR CREDIT AS A REFUSAL OFTEN OFFENDS"

It was during the first couple of years or so of my employment with Law, Russell's that I visited, along with Alan Gostick, the Playhouse, which I understood was possibly the First Temperance Hall in England. It was in Chapel Street and was formerly called Jowett Hall as a tribute to the Socialist worker of that time. I think that following a fire and some re-building it was re-named the Civic Theatre, and later The Bradford Playhouse and Film Theatre. More recently it became the J.B. Priestley Playhouse and Film Theatre and suffered another serious fire in 1996.

Some very well-known actors and actresses began their careers on the stage of the old "Civic", under the direction of Esme Church and others. I have some very happy memories of appearing on the stage of the "Civic" with Busby's Amateur Dramatic Society and one of the plays that we performed was "Daddy Longlegs" but I cannot now remember with any degree of certainty whether it was at the "Civic" or at the old "Southgate Hall" for I remember appearing with Busby's at each of them.

One of my abiding memories is that of seeing the "Telegram Boys" or "Messengers" riding about the streets of the city mounted on their red bicycles. The telegram was the normal means of communication where urgent matters such as Shipping Instructions, Offers for Sale or Purchase were involved. On these occasions, when the office-boys were called to "ANSWER THE BELL" it might well be to receive at the hands of a "Telegram Boy" a telegram, or it might be a Cablegram from abroad, brought by one of the messengers of the "CABLE & WIRELESS CO." or from "THE WESTERN UNION TELEGRAPH CO.".

The fact that we had frequently to take a telegram to the Post Office and hand it over for onward transmission, reminds me of another of those incidents that I would prefer to forget! I know that I hadn't been at LR's very long, but I had been given a telegram to take to the G.P.O. and the intention was that I should perform this small task at the same time as taking the mail-bag to the Box Office in Forster Square. It was one of my "nightschool" evenings and so when the mail was finished I went along with the bag to the G.P.O. and then back to the office for a cup of tea, after which I went off to my class.

We were half-way through the session when, putting my hand into my pocket, I positively froze when my fingers encountered a folded telegram form! I couldn't get away soon enough, but it must have been getting on for half past nine when I reached the G.P.O., which at that time of course, was all locked up! "What am I to do now?" I said to myself. The only course of action that suggested itself was to go round to the back of the building and see if I could find just one person who would be sympathetic towards me in my predicament. Perhaps I was more fortunate than I deserved to be, for I did find such a person who accepted my telegram with good grace, to my great relief! Fortunately, once again, I was never made aware of any repercussions, but I am sure that I never made that particular blunder again all the time I was at Law Russell's.

Across the Counting House, and between the desks of the invoice typists and the Petty Cashier was another desk on which rested a number of wooden filing cabinets with slide-top openings and they were so full and heavy that in that condition they simply could not be moved! I hardly ever saw anyone refer to these records, but I subsequently learnt that they were the results of status enquiries concerning companies who wished to do business with LR's. There were a number of companies who specialised in supplying this kind of information, in addition to the banks. Bradstreets British was such a firm, and the one with which I was most familiar.

I used to visit Bradstreets British quite regularly in order to take a letter which contained an application form for this type of status enquiry. Bradstreets' office was in Cheapside, almost opposite the Midland Hotel. I used to like going there to hand in a letter because usually the "Enquiries" window would be opened by a lovely girl of about sixteen years of age, with round, rosy cheeks, jet black hair and a nice cheerful approach. We used to smile shyly at each other, and I looked forward to the return visit when she would come to our "Enquiries" window with the reply to our enquiry, when again we could share our blushing smiles. Sad to relate, however, the budding romance came to an end, never having been nurtured by either of us!

I was born in Low Moor, where I lived for more than thirty years, in several different houses. During my time at Law, Russell's, and for a number of years afterwards, we lived in the delightful hamlet of Moor Top which is situated just beyond Harold Park and adjoining the North Bierley Cemetery. It was a great area in which to spend one's early years, with lots of open spaces and with farms and fields, cattle and horses. There were several reservoirs and ponds, large and small where boys could fish to their heart's content; there were also streams galore in which to paddle and sail home-made boats! There was everything to satisfy the needs and healthy pursuits of growing lads, in summer or winter time. This was, of course, before the council estates ate up the woodlands, the open fields and the farm's occupied by the Dysons, the Hughes and the Scotts.

When I started to work in the City I never considered it to be any hardship to have to walk such a long way down to Huddersfield Road in order to catch a tram; nor did I think that the walk back was any problem, even on dark winter evenings. After all, I had been doing this kind of thing during the previous ten years or so, and it was second nature to me as it was to my family and friends. In those days, the possibility of being attacked was considered to be remote and I don't recall that I ever heard of anyone being held up and robbed, "mugged", to use today's expression.

There were very few cars on the roads by comparison with today's traffic and tramcars were the principal means of travel to and from the city. As a consequence, there were quite long queues in the city at the end of the day, and the trams were generally quite full at these times as they were in a morning as well. The trams were far less comfortable than buses are today! There were no upholstered seats in those days; usually just plain, ribbed wooden seats. On a very cold morning if you did get a seat, you hoped that it would be one that had just been vacated, otherwise it was likely to be extremely cold sitting! Cold comfort you might have called it! I do think though, that as the years went by there was a gradual improvement in the comfort that was offered by the trams.

I recall an occasion when I caught a tram at Low Moor in order to go to work. I don't think there was any snow about at the time, but I do remember that it was a very cold morning indeed. When the tram arrived at the Victoria Square tram-stop, the lower saloon was already full and it was a case of "UPSTAIRS ONLY". Unfortunately, it was the type, as most of them were, that did not have a fully enclosed upper deck, each end being roofed but otherwise exposed to the elements. There were sliding doors across each end which protected the passengers who were fortunate enough to be seated inside, but those who were sitting, or even standing outside at the front or at the back had little protection from the weather, and on a very cold or wet morning the journey could be extremely unpleasant. As a matter of fact, I have not forgotten such an experience which was mine whilst travelling at the back of a tram of this type.

It was early morning and I was on my way to work when suddenly, instead of being on my feet, I found myself on the floor with the conductor looking into my face, rubbing my hands and working my arms up and down. I can see him now, though he must have died many years ago. He was a local man, whom I had known as a tram conductor some years earlier when I was attending Wyke Council School. It must have taken a moment or two for me to "come round" and for a little while I couldn't think where I was. In spite of having had a good breakfast (and my dad always saw to it that I had a good breakfast with which to face the day), it became apparent to me that I must have fainted from the cold! By the time that the tram arrived in Town Hall Square I was feeling more like myself again and so I got off and just carried on as usual to the office. I remember thinking afterwards that it had never occurred to me to go straight back home. That's how important a job was in those days!

As a junior I had to carry out the duties of errand boy quite often during my first year or so, and I was required to visit many of our local suppliers of printed material and so forth, most of whom have long since gone out of business. In fact, the number of people around who remember some of the firms that I used to visit must now be quite small!

One of the places that I used to visit occasionally was the firm of Alf. Smith & Co., Printers of Scoresby Street, I think it was. We used to be supplied with quite a lot of printed material by them, though I cannot now remember what kind it was. It could have been letterheads, invoice forms or just printed envelopes. I thought that they might have gone out of businesses as I hadn't heard of Alf. Smith's for a long time until quite recently when I came across an item in the Telegraph & Argus to the effect that the firm had been acquired by the Leeds printing group of Hunters. Further enquiries revealed that after leaving Little Germany, Alf. Smith's had occupied premises in Wibsey, but also that they had moved from those premises to the ones which they now occupy in Brighouse Road, Low Moor; within half a mile of my home, and I didn't know it!

Another printer whom I visited occasionally was a Mr. Sheard. I can't recall where his works were as I was unable to call more than a few times because, sadly, no doubt due to the worry of a declining business, he took his own life, I think at the Strid at Bolton Abbey. I also recall that we used to have some printing work carried out by Ernest Cummins, whose works were in Bolton Road. There were one or two other firms in the city centre that I visited from time to time; one of these was Harrison &

Co., Stationers, whose works were in the Charles Street or Hall Ings area. I suppose we obtained a variety of stationery items from them, but I can only remember taking back empty stone ink bottles, for which we were given a few coppers. We used a large quantity of ink, mostly for filling ink-wells, and as a consequence we used plenty of blotting paper as well, which I suppose would also be supplied by Harrisons.

CHAPTER FIVE

We Smell A Rat

I now digress and return to the subject of the Law, Russell building which incidentally, at the time of writing was occupied by the Department of Social Security; I must say that since my first acquaintance with this building I have come to understand just a little more about the importance of natural lighting and the emphasis that was placed upon it, in the design of the premises at 63, Vicar Lane. When I first began to work there, I had no standards at all by which to judge the excellence or otherwise of the buildings in Little Germany, but my time as an office-worker in the area helped me to understand something of the qualities which made the Law, Russell building, for me at any rate, outstanding in an area which is recognised by experts as abounding in notable examples of the skill of the architect and the builder.

Mr. Roberts, in his booklet "Little Germany" makes particular reference to the important place that is occupied by natural lighting. Working in the Counting House on the ground floor, as I did for several years, I could see at a glance some of the steps that had been taken to improve the natural lighting of this, as well as other parts of the building. Although I had never seen this feature in a building before, and this is not surprising since I had virtually no knowledge at all of the buildings in Little Germany, and especially of the interiors of such buildings, but I was immediately impressed by the "Well-light". a square opening around which, on each floor were mahogany tables or counters for the laying-out of pieces. Natural lighting was provided to each floor by the attic windows at the very top of the buildings as well as in the usual manner from the windows in the outer walls.

When I was making these notes I felt sure that during the alterations that took place within the building nearly twenty years ago, the well-light would have disappeared. I have since been able to verify that my assumption was correct. The huge "hole" which extended from the top to the first floor is to be seen no more, having been sealed off, but whether the floors have been extended to cover the opening and block off each floor completely, I do not know. Certainly the well-light, although giving much-needed natural light to each floor was, without doubt, a great fire risk and I am fairly certain that this feature of warehouse design is now thing of the past, as are some other steps that were taken to improve the natural lighting of warehouses and offices! I have noticed though, that the external well of the loading bay is still in existence, with its walls lined with the old, and now rather dingy-looking white (?) tiles!

One rather striking effort was made to improve the natural lighting of the Counting House which I cannot recall having seen on any other building in the city, with the exception of the old and much-loved "Swan Arcade". As far as the Law, Russell building was concerned it was obviously hoped that improved natural lighting would be achieved by suspending quite large mirrors outside the windows in Vicar Lane. The mirrors, which were as wide as the windows, but only half as long, were suspended on a couple of chains at an angle of approximately forty-five degrees so as to reflect as much light as was available into the ground-floor offices. Although I worked in those offices I cannot remember whether in fact, the system was very efficient.

An occasion comes to mind when Alan Gostick and I were working late one evening. As far as we knew there was no one else in the building. Dick Boulton had done his rounds and everywhere was locked up for the night. He left with us the responsibility for locking the front door as we left, leaving everything secure and then taking the keys to the Town Hall, which Dick normally did each evening. We were working away quietly, with hardly a sound to be heard, when we became aware of a rustling noise, rather like the sound of papers being leafed through. It seemed to emanate from further up the office from where we were working, and as we believed that we were alone in the building, it was clear that the sound would have to be investigated. To begin with, our considered opinion was that it was the sound of mice in a waste-paper basket, but was it mice? Might it not be RATS!!!

We crept along towards the origin of the sound, which now seemed to be in the vicinity of Mr. Dodgson's office. We each grabbed a heavy round ruler and stood there without making a sound - just listening! I didn't feel very brave just at that moment, but Alan wasn't noted for his bravery under fire, either, though I seem to recall that he was urging me forward - from behind! Somehow we pushed open the door of Mr. Dodgson's office and with our rulers at the ready we prepared to fight off any attack from the waste-paper basket! Not a movement, not a sound; and then as we stood there, beginning to breathe just slightly, we heard it! Scratch, scratch, scratch!!

Together our eyes were drawn upwards to the window, and it was then that we realised that the sound, whatever it was, was coming from OUTSIDE. Only then did we discover the cause of all our apprehension. One of the chains that supported the mirror outside the office had become detached at the bottom and because of the slight breeze blowing at the time, it was swinging back and forth across the face of the mirror, making a scratching sound in the process. This was the noise that had been so hard to identify, so then, after successfully completing our mission, we gladly went back to work!

Dick Bolton was a character and no mistake! He was not very tall, but quite broad-shouldered and strong, with very bowed legs. We used to say, but not in his hearing, that "He couldn't stop a pig in a passage!" No one would have said that he was very handsome, either. Rugged-looking, yes, very and with a powerful voice to match! I can't remember what his main job was, perhaps he was a percher or a packer but he was responsible for locking-up and taking the keys to the police at the Town Hall each evening. At first he "nearly frightened me to death", as the saying goes, with his loud voice, which seemed quite natural for him, as did his broken and badly stained teeth and his foul-smelling pipe! But he was really one of the best! His approach was often like the advance of a thunder-storm, but it was just an act. I can see him now, sitting on one of the stools at the end of the desk opposite to Fred Pawson. While we lads got on with the job of finishing off mail, Dick would be sitting there, smoking and haranguing Fred, who was always the last of the senior clerks to leave at night, but equally, he was always the last to arrive in a morning as well!

Dick Bolton was, I believe, a very active member of the Bradford Cinderella Club. I don't know if he held any kind of executive position, but I do know that he did a lot of good work for the deprived children of the city, and his rough exterior hid a heart of pure gold!

One particular morning, although I can't remember the date, important though it was, but some time after the departure of Mr. James, the whole of the Counting House staff was called together, to be addressed by Mr. Arthur Hitt, who was at that time, I think, the Managing Director of the company. As far as I can recall, the gist of his remarks was to the effect that, unknown to us, we had all been sacked by Law, Russell & Co. Ltd., and re-engaged by the new company that was to manage affairs in the future, under the direction of a Receiver and Manager!

It must have been about this time, or perhaps even a little before this dramatic announcement was made, that I was summoned to the "ENQUIRY" window by the ringing of the bell. Standing there was a very large, important-looking gentleman who obviously believed in making himself heard! In a loud voice, which I was sure Mr. Hitt would be able to hear in the private office, he announced "MR HITT, PLEASE - MR SHARP!!!" It was Mr. James Sharp of Shirley Manor, Wyke, and of the Bradford Dyer's Association Ltd. I didn't know what effect he had on Mr. Hitt when I showed him into the private office but I had heard something of his business reputation, and he made me tremble! I felt sorry for Mr. Hitt if we owed them a lot of money, and in the light of subsequent events, I'm sure that we did!

As I continue to look back, it now seems to me that some of the methods employed were somewhat out-dated and sometimes rather extravagant even for those days, but they were typical of procedures that had remained unaltered over a number of years. The Sales Day Books were, as I recall, bright red in colour, about half-an-inch thick, and every one needed to have its own departmental number stamped upon it in gold leaf! I had to go along now and then to B.F. Hardwick & Co., (another firm who, I believe were in the Charles Street area), either to take a book to be stamped, or to collect a book that had been stamped with its appropriate number. My one clear recollection of visiting Hardwick's works was the smell! There it goes again - my sense of smell must be very sensitive! The smell at Hardwick's was the smell of hot glue, which is not at all surprising since they were bookbinders!

I was not particularly impressed by a piece of equipment that I learned to use. For some reason which I never understood, it had its abode on the second floor, outside the offices of the Fancy Room. As a schoolboy I had often found myself using a copying-ink pencil. They were always "VENUS" pencils. I am not sure what the attraction of this type of pencil was, unless it was the fact that if you gave the point a few licks, you could get the blue ink all over your fingers, and on to your face too, without much effort! You could make notes, draw pictures, in fact you could do lots of useful things with a well-licked pencil - all on the back of your hands!

However, I am sure that I never understood what the real purpose of the copying ink pencil was, until that moment when I was shown how to use the press upstairs. Then the connection between the copying ink pencil and the copier became clearer. Under the instructions of Stanley Robertshaw, I learned to use this relic of former days. Why it was still in use I couldn't imagine! For some reason which wasn't clear to me at the time, and is even less clear to me now, certain documents were hand-written in copying ink, not with a pencil however, but with pen and ink - COPYING INK!

When we were given these particular documents to copy, the procedure was as far as I remember, to take the documents along with a special book, rather like an old-fashioned photograph album, together with a can of water and a paste brush. We opened the book, the leaves of which were of tissue paper, and proceeded to wet quite thoroughly the next leaves to be used, so one had to be most careful when lifting the top leaf, before placing underneath it the document(s) to be copied!

I believe that if there were two or three documents to be copied, they could all be placed in the book at the same time, provided that the required number of leaves had been soaked with water. Then, after closing the book carefully, it was placed between the plates of the press and the top plate was screwed down by means of the cast-iron arms, which turned around a central screw. After a few minutes, when the pressure was released, the book was removed and a copy of the document(s) would remain in the book! Hey Presto! So that was what copying-ink was for; but I am surprised that the method was still in use, even in 1927!

CHAPTER SIX

An Accident And A Romance

I mentioned earlier that the passenger lift was on the left of the front entrance. It was operated by a uniformed member of the Corps of Commissionaires, but all the juniors however, soon learned how to drive the lift, mostly after hours when the bosses were away. As youngsters will, we did play about with it a little bit, and did rather silly things, though not I think, anything that was really dangerous.

There was a wire rope, which ran from the top to the bottom of the lift shaft. This was provided in case of emergency, so that the lift could be stopped at any time and anywhere, even between floors, simply by pulling on the rope, which could easily be grasped from the staircase. So, if one's colleague was taking the lift up or down, the fun was to bring the lift to a halt between floors, and there he would have to remain until you chose to release him! It wasn't a very dangerous thing to do, but it was rather silly, as we came to realise as we grew older.

There was also a goods hoist at the back of the building. I am not sure about this, but I think there may have been two, side by side. Although the goods hoist was intended mainly for the movement of pieces, it was used by everyone on occasion, and we juniors used the works lift quite often when going about our normal duties.

Mention of the goods hoist reminds me of an unpleasant incident which occurred in connection with it. I was going about my duties somewhere out of the office when I received a message to say that I was wanted urgently in the directors' dining room, as Harry had had an accident. Harry Emmett was the junior office-boy at the time, so he was probably only just about seventeen years of age.

When I reached the dining room, it was to find a policeman and several anxious-looking members of staff standing around the large mahogany dining table, and Harry lying there with one shoe missing. He had been using the goods lift and somehow, whether accidentally or carelessly (I don't think I ever found out), had put his foot a little way through the gate, with disastrous results for he suffered a broken, or at least a badly lacerated big toe! He was off work for some months. I know that I used to visit him straight from the office, about once a week for a while. He lived with his parents in Christopher Terrace, Little Horton.

They were always pleased to see me when I called, and would usually have a meal ready for me, in spite of the fact that things were becoming more and more difficult, and the cost of living was continuing to rise! I believe though that Harry's father was in full-time work, but I can't remember what his job was; perhaps he had a manual job such as that of a mechanic or an engineer, because I seem to recollect that he wore overalls.

My mind goes back to the time when I was visiting Harry during his period of convalescence. Sometimes when he was beginning to feel rather better after his ordeal, he used to play for me. I know that my own piano playing wasn't anything to write home about at that time (it is non-existent now!), but Harry's was worse! I can only remember one tune - but it was the accompaniment to a supposedly "popular" song of the day. The lyric was paltry and the tune - you could hardly call it a melody - was even worse! Here are the first few lines, and fortunately they are all I can remember :

> "I scream, you scream
> We all scream for ice-cream
> Ra! Ra!! Ra!!!"

Wonderful, Marvellous!! But my guess is that it didn't get into the "Top-Ten" that year! There was a lot of that kind of stuff about though, at the time!

Thinking about Harry and his accident caused me to start thinking again about the directors' dining room at Law, Russell's, To begin with, the kitchen was "below stairs" and it could be reached from the dining room by means of the steps, which were rather steep, and which led down from the corner of the room. It could also be reached from a door on the outside in Vicar Lane, just on the bend. Mrs Weston was the cook; a dark-haired young woman with a neat and tidy appearance. She came each day to prepare a meal for about ten or a dozen directors and senior staff. She used to arrive in the kitchen after having spent some time in the city, visiting various suppliers and leaving her orders for meat and vegetables etc., which, I suppose, were for delivery the following day, in most cases.

I was often required to visit the dining room while a meal was in progress, to take in a telegram, or to ask one of the diners to the telephone. At such times the smell - there it goes again! - the smell was very distinctive and I soon learned to recognise it as a mixture of the smells of bottled beer, Stilton Cheese and cigars! Needless to say, at the end of the meal the room was thick with smoke!

One of the very first jobs I had to learn was how to make the directors' coffee. Stanley of course was the expert and I had to learn the skill from him. I suppose it would be about ten o'clock each morning that the two of us used to leave the vicinity of the office desk and after sending out the general call "Answer the bell, please", we used to disappear through the dining room and down the steps to the kitchen, where we proceeded to start making the directors' coffee!

We used to fill one large saucepan with milk, and a similar sized pan with water, and then we scattered a quantity of coffee (I've forgotten how much) on top of the water, and brought both pans almost, but not quite, to the boil. I think we must then have turned off the gas underneath both pans and left everything for Mrs. Weston to complete and serve at the usual time. I find it difficult to imagine that we did all this without making a cup for ourselves, but I have no recollection of our doing so. Perhaps we preferred that it should not interfere with our visit to "Ma Rogan's" for our tea and "Tram stoppers" at around eleven o'clock!

A kettle-full of water was always left in the hearth for the making of the directors' tea, and I recall that their choice was China tea! I had never tasted China tea before, but I soon got used to it! At the end of the day, and before we went off to the G.P.O. or to Evening Classes, we always made ourselves a cup of tea, and as a result we soon became addicted to China tea!

The office-cleaner came in each morning, usually to sweep the floors, mop out the toilets and dust the desks. Her name was Mrs. Cook - a well built woman, rather short in stature. She lived up Bolton Road, and I seem to recall that sometimes she would bring her small daughter with her. Perhaps that was during school holidays as she would be about six years of age, I suppose, so if the daughter is still living she will now be in her seventies, I expect.

I have mentioned the Grey Room several times, without mentioning the staff. There were just two of them - the Grey Room Manager, Mr. Briggs, and his assistant Harry Robinson. Mr. Briggs was a rather short man, with black hair and black, bushy eyebrows. He wore the somewhat deep, stiff collars that were beginning to disappear entirely from the well-dressed man's apparel! He usually seemed to be making entries in a huge book, which presumably was the record of the movement of the grey pieces to and from the dyers. I recall that because of his small stature he stood on a platform about six inches high, to enable him to reach his stock-book in comfort! His deputy, Harry Robinson, on the other hand, managed very well without the use of the platform. Harry was as different from Mr. Briggs as could be imagined. Mr. Briggs was short, Harry was tall; Mr. Briggs had a very dark sort of complexion, but Harry with his fresh complexion simply glowed with good health like a man whose life has been spent in the sunshine and fresh air of the countryside such as a farm worker, for instance! In spite of all their dissimilarities they seemed to work quite well together, and I am sure that they, more than any of us, were well aware of a decline in the amount of work passing through the Grey Room!

Sometimes when things were a bit slack, or perhaps during our lunch break, Alan and I would go down to the basement and have a good look around. This was not the Blanket Department, but the section that was used for the storage of various items. On one of these exploratory ventures we came across an old typewriter which we rescued from its "unmarked grave" and later after spending some time on it with a screwdriver and an oil can I eventually got it to perform with some degree of reliability, but it was hardly up to the standard of the machines that we were then using in the Counting House.

It was an old "Monarch", with a 14" carriage and I thought that if I had such a machine at home I would be able to make very good use of it, so I asked Mr. Leach if it would be possible for me to buy this old machine from the company. His answer was "Yes, can you manage £2?" I thought the price was most satisfactory and I became the proud owner of a long carriage typewriter. It was a very heavy machine; I had a real struggle to get it down to the tram, where I was able to put it on the platform, near to the driver.

It was a good investment, even better than I realised at the time of purchase, for later, when I had become unemployed and had great difficulty in finding employment, I did manage to get a job of sorts, working as a traveller for a firm in Cheapside named Hirst & Co., who sold and repaired typewriters and other office equipment. I wasn't very good as a typewriter salesman, and needless to say, after one week Mr Hirst indicated that if I couldn't bring off a few sales he would be compelled to let me go!

Fortunately for me, in my brief spell with the firm I had become on good terms with the mechanic, who, when he knew that I was leaving, informed me that he would be happy to take a look at my typewriter and give it a good overhaul if I could get it down to his workshop before I left. This was obviously too good a chance to miss, and as a result I left the firm after just two weeks, as an unsuccessful salesman, but with a typewriter which was now in pretty good condition, if not very modern! This machine subsequently earned me far more than it had cost me, doing typing work - sketches and plays - for other church groups, and my own church's drama activities.

While thinking about the days that have gone, and I suppose most old people do this, we think about the people with whom we worked, people whose influence helped to mould our characters and make us into the sort of folk that we have become, and we wonder how many of these former colleagues, whom we haven't seen for many years, are still living?

It must have been a year or two after I had started work at Law, Russell's that two young ladies came to join us. I can only assume that they came to take the places, as invoice typists, of some of the lads who were a bit older than I was, such as Willie

38

Clarkson and Kenneth Ainsworth. I can't recall whether they left the firm or whether either, or both of them were transferred to other department. At any rate the two young ladies, named Josephine Brady and Marie Crossley began working in the Counting House with us; perhaps not both together, but certainly within a fairly short space of time.

I think that Alan Gostick and I were the very last of the clerical staff to leave when the firm finally ceased trading, and it is possible that both the young ladies left the firm some weeks before we did. I don't think I heard anything at all about Miss Brady after she left. We always used to call her "Jo" but I recall an occasion when she told us that, because she was a Catholic, she had been given the names Josephine, Maria, Romella - and I hope she wasn't pulling our legs. It is strange though, isn't it, how such unimportant trifles are remembered when more important items are forgotten?

I was aware that a close friendship had been blossoming for some time between Marie and a young man who worked upstairs; a young man of whom I had the greatest regard, named Herbert Bearpark. We were quite friendly, without being really close friends. He was a bit older than me and I believe he worked for Mr. Batchelor in the Plain Department on the first floor. He used to sell chocolate on behalf of his church, not in a very big way, but he used to keep a few bars in his drawer, and I used to go up to buy one now and then. He had a nose operation whilst he was working at Law, Russell's. I don't know where the information came from, it's such a long time ago, but perhaps I read the announcement in the "Telegraph" to the effect that he and Marie had married. I also heard with regret when he died some years later. As I had been thinking of those days so long ago, I wondered whether or not she was still living!

I couldn't get this question out of my mind, when I was working on these memoirs, and eventually, I decided that the only course to take was for me to telephone Canon Bearpark at Steeton, and get the true facts. I had met him a number of years ago at a Low Moor Council of Churches gathering, and as we talked, I was able to confirm that Herbert Bearpark was his father.

I spoke with him on the telephone just recently, when he confirmed that his father was quite a young man when he died in 1955 at the age of forty six. I was pleased to hear however, that his mother, Marie, was reasonably well, bearing in mind the fact that she had just celebrated her eightieth birthday, though she is not getting about very often these days owing to problems with her legs. She lives on her own at Guiseley and he felt sure that she would welcome either a visit or a telephone call from me. As a result I had the great pleasure of speaking on the telephone with Marie, more than sixty years after we had last had any contact with each other! It was a conversation which gave me much pleasure, and I hope that it brought some equally pleasant memories back to Marie as well. Sadly she died in September 1994.

These recollections bring back other memories, and I am somehow reminded of the many times when Alan and I resorted to the Grey Room, and after lunch we had a session playing our flageolets (or tin whistles) together. We had discovered that we could both get a tune out of this instrument, so what could be more natural than that we should play a few duets? I was a budding tenor singer and a failed pianist, so we were able to play a few favourite tunes - mostly hymn tunes and folk tunes - in two part harmony! We were told that the sound of our playing could be heard practically throughout the whole building! I remember Marie saying, after one of our renderings of the hymn tune "Deep Harmony" by Handel Parker, that this was her favourite hymn tune. I wonder if it is still a favourite tune? It doesn't appear to me that it is as popular as once it was. I fear that this is a fate that many of today's popular hymns and tunes will also suffer in due course.

CHAPTER SEVEN

The Melody Lingers On

I can't remember just when it happened, but the firm of William Berry & Co. Ltd., Lining Merchants, whose premises were at 13, Currer Street, came to join us at 63, Vicar Lane, and were incorporated with Law, Russell & Co. Ltd., There was Mr. Berry himself, his secretary Miss Mitchell (I believe she was called Dorothy), and Walter Gadd, who seemed to have such a lot of responsibility for everything to do with Wm. Berry & Co. Ltd., for he worked like a "Trojan", but all to no avail unfortunately as it turned out!

It has occurred to me lately that the name "LITTLE GERMANY" for the business area roughly between Church Bank and East Parade, was hardly ever used in conversation, during the time that I worked in the area, even though the name had originated many years earlier, in the 1860's. I do remember though, that my father gave me the explanation, which was commonly accepted at the time, why the area was so called.

When German textile merchants set up their businesses in Bradford, they established a close-knit community in the area which is now far more widely known than was formerly the case, as "LITTLE GERMANY". I understand though that the real explanation for the name is much more complex! Be that as it may, a great publicity effort has gone into making the area much more widely appreciated. It is now recognised by far more people than ever before, as one of the city's treasures and an area of outstanding historical interest, one that should be preserved. I trust that as a city we have learned the lesson of our former mistakes, with regard to protecting our heritage.

The name of Alan Gostick keeps cropping up in this narrative. After working as colleagues for a couple of years or so, we had become quite good friends, and one or two promotions brought me closer to him in the "pecking order"! In fact, by the time that the liquidation of the company was taking place, Alan was Senior Clerk and I was next in seniority on that side of the office.

Alan and I had become close friends both in the office and in some of our outside activities. We visited each other's homes occasionally, and got to know each other's family quite well. I discovered that I had known Alan's brother Geoffrey quite well, when we were both schoolboys attending Grange Road Secondary School. He was a few years younger than I was, but I knew him as a boy who was always smiling and who, once a week, worked on the next bench to me in the woodwork class, where two different age groups shared the department at the same time.

One of Alan's sisters worked for a firm who occupied premises at the very top of a building in the city centre. Many people will remember the building at the junction of Town Hall Square and Tyrrel Street, and at the end of the block which faced up Great Horton Road. I think the ground-floor shop premises were occupied by Burtons the Tailors. Well, the top floor was occupied by this "PORTRAIT ARTIST", whose name was writ large across the windows - DENIS R. THOMPSON - beneath a skylight which, because it was painted bright green, always attracted my attention, and that of other people too, as they approached the city centre from the direction of Manchester Road.

It must have been due to the influence of his sister that Alan joined Thompson's on a part-time basis, and then after some months I, too, went to work for them. In those days even a few shillings extra each week was quite an incentive, but at the beginning I didn't realise how much work was involved. I was given the Shipley, Saltaire and Thackley areas in which to collect weekly payments for pictures and, looking back, it does seem that I had to do an awful lot of walking on Friday evenings and Saturday afternoons, just to earn a "few bob"! The system employed was that a canvasser would be sent round a certain district requesting family photographs for enlarging, colouring and framing; payment to be made on a weekly basis. These orders, I noticed, seemed to come from the very poorest of families and more often than not, an order would be for the enlargement of a photograph of the deceased parent of either husband or wife.

I remember visiting an older woman, whether married or single, I cannot remember, but I know that she was always alone if I was fortunate enough to catch her in, so she was probably a widow. She lived in a not very pleasant area of Shipley at that time - Dale Street! If I found her at home, and sober, on a Friday evening I was extremely lucky; even so, it might take three weekly visits to collect just one shilling (5p). Sometimes she would greet me with a kind of affectionate hug; at other times, when she was reeking of gin and with a carving knife in her hand, I used to fear for my life and with good reason!

It couldn't last! Sometimes on a hot Saturday afternoon, I used to spend a large part of the commission that I would receive on ice-cold lemonade and ice-cream, as I trudged wearily from street to street. It didn't last!! Eventually the call of the tennis court and the cricket field became too strong and I handed in my resignation!

When I was in my early teens I went on holiday with my parents and my sister Evelyn, who was four years my junior. This was a great treat for us all, for my parents couldn't manage the expense of a holiday every year. Amongst all the other exciting activities available in Blackpool at that time were the visits we paid to the demonstrations that were held in the open-fronted booths on the Golden Mile, in the Olympia and the Winter Gardens. There was generally a man or a woman at the piano, and a much younger man who was the singer-cum salesman. They were surrounded by counters (it was often a circular booth) on which were displayed dozens and dozens of copies of popular songs. My sister and I used to stand and gaze in ecstasy as the young man sang a song and then went into his "spiel" about the merits and the price of the song that he had just been singing. I had forgotten how much we used to pay for a single copy and I thought it might have been 1/- (5p) for a copy containing the words and music of the choruses only, of up to twenty songs for 2/6d (12.5p). In fact, when I was on holiday recently at a Methodist holiday hotel, I came across a couple of these ancient copies. One was called "LAWRENCE WRIGHT'S 39TH SONG AND DANCE ALBUM" 1/- NET, and the other had the title "LAWRENCE WRIGHT'S 1ST MONSTER ALBUM OF FOX-TROT SONGS" - PRICE 6d. These were collections of songs that the publisher hoped would become popular, but in my experience most of them never did! Nevertheless, my sister and I both enjoyed these visits to the music booths, which our parents just endured, as parents do! On one occasion we came away from one of these demonstrations with a copy of a song called "HALFWAY TO HEAVEN". Who, except me remembers the song today? Very few I imagine! My sister used to struggle through the accompaniment on the piano, while I did the same on the ukulele, singing at the same time! It wasn't a great song, but it kept us out of mischief for months!

We used to buy those copies of popular music, from time to time, and we always had one or two about the house, so that we could have a sing-song when a few friends got together. Some of these collections lasted from one generation to the next, as did the copies I came across, which someone must have taken away with them and happily left in the hotel! I remember quite distinctly the title of such a song from a previous decade, it was called "TILL THE SANDS OF THE DESERT GROW COLD". We used to sing it quite often when we were young. I can't remember any of the words now - "But the melody lingers on"!

As I continue to look back, I recall many, many happy days. There were, of course, some sad ones as well, and for some people there seemed to be far too many sad days!

We were living in times that were often rather difficult, even in our own household. Money for the absolute necessities of life was always found, but for clothes and holidays, it was often a real struggle. Although my father was never unemployed to my knowledge, he wouldn't be overpaid at the B.D.A., and with a wife and two children to support it was often a struggle. Compared with some families in our neighbourhood however, we had a fairly comfortable existence. One family in particular comes to mind who, I'm sure, never knew where the next meal was coming from!

This was made clear to me one day when I was playing beside the lake in Harold Park, Low Moor. A lad who was a member of this very poor family came up to me and, knowing that my home was only a few yards way, just the other side of the park wall (we rarely used the gates), asked if I would get him a slice of bread! Not a bacon sandwich mark you, or even a jam sandwich, but a slice of bread! So times were very hard in that household, though I am sure that the father's drinking habits didn't help matters!

There were, in the twenties and thirties many families like this, who found that life was really hard, and when we think of conditions today, with unemployment on the three million mark, we have to recognise that for the average householder conditions today are generally far better than they were at the turn of the century, and have been all the years since!

Although we had our financial problems at home when my sister and I were young, it was impossible for us not to notice the families who were really poor, and other families who had problems of one sort or another. Certain unfortunate incidents come to mind which I am not sure that I should include in these reminiscences, but I will try to tell the truth briefly and without being morbid about such things.

Living as we did, between the two large expanses of water which were Royds Hall dam and Harold Park lake, we were bound to notice that these places seemed to attract a large number of suicides! Often, though not always, they were people who lived locally. Although I wouldn't like to give the impression that these cries of despair occurred regularly, they did occur often enough for adults, and young people too, to enquire "Have you noticed that they are dragging the dam again?" This sometimes meant that the park lake was being referred to, but more frequently it was Royds Hall dam that was the scene of the tragedy, and this meant that the police, having transported a boat from the park to Royds Hall dam, were rowing back and forth across the dam, dragging grappling irons behind the boat in search for the body of a suicide.

Perhaps the police search was instituted as a result of a note having been left indicating the person's intentions. I could name at lest three people who committed suicide on one or other of the two lakes, and of course, over the years there were unfortunately, many more. I suspect that Royds Hall dam was chosen more often because of the fact that it was further from public thoroughfares and so there was less chance of the action being observed. My own grandfather committed suicide in Royds Hall dam, a few years before I was born; I never knew the reason for his despair, but I do have a copy of the Death Certificate which certifies that he "Drowned himself while in a state of temporary insanity". Small comfort to the family which was fairly large, with two boys and three girls, making a family of seven! I believe that many such tragedies occurred as a result of the stress suffered by the heads of these families, and brought on by the hard times in which they were living. Incidentally, the column in the newspaper which recorded the inquest was headed "BRADFORD SUICIDES", which seems to say something about life (and death!) in those hard times!

On looking back through these memoirs, I realise that I have not yet mentioned the names of two other boys who came to work on the office desk at Law, Russell's. One of these was Bill Adams, a rather stocky lad, with a "Geordie" accent. I think he must have joined us when Stanley Robertshaw was transferred to the Entering Room. At any rate, that was when I became senior office boy. I soon discovered that the work involved was not exactly what Bill had in mind for his first job. He made it quite clear to me that he thought that he was meant for something better and I'm sure he wouldn't have minded my saying this! It was a struggle just to get him to appreciate the joys of shared experiences! I don't know how long he stayed with us, but I suspect that it was no more than a few months at the most. His sense of co-operation became less and less. In the end I was compelled to inform Mr. Leach of the situation when Bill began to take himself off home before we had finished the mail! I didn't know whether Bill decided to depart for pastures new or whether he was requested to look in that direction, but he left, with no tears from the senior office-boy!

Ronald Dixon was a different type of lad altogether. He probably joined us as a result of being an acquaintance of Alan Gostick. I think they were both brought up in the Shearbridge area of the city, and both attended the Shearbridge Wesleyan Sunday School there. Ronald was a grand lad; big, blonde and very strong. You knew that he was a lad to be relied on, that he would go places and make his mark in the world. Unfortunately, by the time he joined us at Law Russell's he had, I believe, lost both his parents, and as he had been their only son, it meant that life for him became very hard indeed. I think he was living with an Aunt and Uncle somewhere in the Undercliffe district of the city, and although he must have missed a lot of the affection that only loving parents can provide, I don't remember that he ever gave an indication of a sense of loss!

At the time that Law, Russell's closed down, Ronald and I were little more than colleagues, friendly colleagues, but no more. It so happened however that when the end did come for me and when I obtained my first real job after being unemployed for eighteen months, I did get a job at Brown, Muffs in the "Parcel Corner" as it was called then, but I was continually on the look-out for a suitable job of a clerical nature. After six months, such a vacancy arose and I started work at Busby's on Manningham Lane, as a clerk in the office, and later as a bookkeeper.

Now, who should be working for my new employer but my erstwhile colleague Ronald. We were able, not only to resume our friendship, but to cement it! Ronald began to display an interest, and to reveal aspirations quite unconnected with his job at Busbys', and he began to study to become a local preacher in what was by this time The Methodist Church. This was some years before I took the same step myself! I felt then that his aim was to go as far as he could in the field of Christian service! In the end however, he became a policeman and served with great credit in the Leeds City Police Force. I was proud to be a groomsman at his wedding to Joan Lambert, and I was sorry to hear of his death, a few years ago!

CHAPTER EIGHT

Machine All Over

One aspect of the Bradford trade in wool and in piece goods was the number of horse-drawn carts and wagons to be seen going to and fro, carrying with them the distinctive sound of iron-shod hooves on granite setts, as the drivers competed for passage room with many other vehicles which were transporting goods to and from one of the railway stations, of which, in the 1920's there were four - Forster Square, Valley Goods, the Exchange Station and Adolphus Street. There were also on the city streets numerous two-wheeled hand-carts making deliveries of all kinds of supplies to the various offices and warehouses. I recall the name of one such supplier who used this type of transport for making deliveries to Law, Russell's; this was Alf. Smith & Co., whose delivery man used to have to drag his hand-cart loaded with printed stationery up and down those steep streets. I was thankful that such a hard and difficult task was not mine!

So often the work of the heavy draught horse became somewhat dangerous and the risk of slipping and falling on the steep Bradford streets was always present, especially in very wet or icy conditions. On one occasion, when I was passing along Thornton Road, I could see a small crowd gathered on the opposite side of the road, at the bottom of Godwin Street, where it meets Thornton Road. It looked as though a railway delivery wagon had just come down the slope and was turning into Thornton Road when the horse slipped and fell.

The accident had already occurred when I came on the scene, and the driver, with considerable assistance from passers-by, I imagine, had succeeded in getting the horse back on to its feet and freed from the shafts. It was a pitiful sight to see the poor animal, as it tried to hold its nearside foot off the ground, and it was trembling violently, no doubt because of the pain and the shock. Its leg was obviously broken and only the arrival of a man with a gun could put an end to the animal's suffering. I felt really sad to see the noble beast in this situation and I couldn't bear to stay to see the end of the unpleasant episode.

I used to be impressed by the "neat and tidy" appearance of the bales of merchandise as they left our premises on the first stage of their journey, in fulfilment of export orders, all with their destination marks stencilled on them in black ink! I had few occasions to visit the Packing Room and then out of curiosity, but it was there that I began to understand the mystery of how the bales were packed, with the aid of the powerful presses, which ensured that the rolls of cloth (or pieces) were packed so tightly together that, once they were enclosed in canvas and stitched up with twine, they were virtually solid masses of textile materials. Bales of wool, on the other hand, could easily be identified when on the carriers' wagons, because they were apparently much less tightly packed than piece goods, and so were more "springy-looking" - that's my expression, but I don't know how else to describe their appearance when compared with bales of textile materials.

Law, Russell's was almost entirely a piece goods, or stuff warehouse, so that vehicles arriving at the loading bay were normally bringing pieces in the grey state from the manufacturer, or bringing pieces which had been dyed and finished. The grey pieces were taken into the "Grey Room" to be recorded as "Grey Stock", and then after a brief examination they were sent on to be dyed and finished. The pieces which were returned after the dyeing and finishing process had been carried out, were taken to the respective departments, viz. : first floor for Plains, Woollens etc., second floor for Fancies, Art. Silks etc., and the third floor for Linings and Umbrella Cloths. The fourth floor , I remember as the Entering Room and part of the floor was also occupied by the Shipping Department where Sydney Catling was in charge.

I find it a little difficult after all this time to remember the location of all the firm's activities, but I think that part of the second floor was occupied by the Pattern Room, at the Field Street side of the building, whilst the London Room was located on the Vicar Lane side of the same floor, where Sydney Catling's brother Willie, was in charge.

I can now only remember the names of three other names of the London Room staff, one of whom was Wilfred Garnett, who came from Low Moor. Wilfred always had, as I recall, a penholder parked on his ear when he was at work, and even when he was walking about. No doubt it was a habit that he had picked up years before, but I did wonder how he managed to get it to stay there all the time; I never could! I believe the other members of the departments were Miss Piercey and Cecil Larrad; I think that Lewis Wood was in charge of the Pattern Room. I used to go to him on the occasions when I required a fent as a dress length for my sister or my mother.

I can remember getting a particular fent which made up into a nice dress for my mother. It was an Art Silk material called "CAMRUSYL" which had the Law, Russell's number of 22579 (we had to type this number so often on Sales Invoices that it isn't surprising that I can still remember it!). I remember too, obtaining another length of material which made up into a lovely coat for my sister, who would be about thirteen or fourteen at the time. The material was a fine worsted called "Apperleen"; I can't remember its number, but I am fairly certain that it was manufactured by George Garnett & Sons Ltd., of Apperley Bridge, hence the name. I've no doubt that I bought many other lengths of material during my time at Law, Russell's but these are the only ones I can remember at the moment!

Although I seem able to remember the names of most of the staff who worked at LRs in the 1920s there are a few cases where I can remember names, even faces, without being able to say just where the owners worked. The names of Lloyd Hitt, Leslie Beard and Miss Jessie Bottomley come readily to mind as members of the Fancy Room staff. I think that Stanley Rushton and possibly Cecil Fox also worked in this department, but in these cases I'm not at all sure, even though I am able to recall what they looked like!

As time passed Alan and I became quite close friends. Perhaps to a few people, especially to my parents, it appeared as though Alan had too much influence over my life, but I think that it was simply that we enjoyed doing the same things together, sometimes rather silly things, it must be admitted, just for fun!

The hairdressing incident is one that must have caused my parents some misgivings. Looking down to Leeds Road from the front door of Law, Russell's one saw on the left corner the Leigh Mills Co.'s premises and immediately opposite was the "Junction" public house which, incidentally, neither of us ever entered! To the left of the "Junction" was a shop which made rubber stamps of all kinds - I've forgotten the name of the owners, but next to them was the hairdresser whose name, I believe was A.E. Light or some similar initials. I should say at this point that Alan's hair was the nondescript type as I'm sure he would have been the first to agree. It just stood up in spikes! Mine, on the other hand, was quite different, thick and curly. Although my parents were proud of it, I grew to hate it and tried my best with Field's Solid Brilliantine to hide the curls and make my hair lie down flat! Any success in this direction was short-lived! Alan came back to the office, having been to the hairdresser's, with locks that were well and truly shorn. I thought that he looked absolutely great! I decided that this was just what I needed, so at the first opportunity Alan and I went down to the hairdresser's. When I was seated in the chair, I remember that the assistant said "How do you want it?" "Like that!" I replied, pointing to Alan's haircut. "Machine all over?" he asked in some surprise, "Yes!" I said as firmly as I thought the occasion required.

I can see now, the look of sheer horror that spread over the faces of my parents when they saw their pride and joy after a "Machine all over"! That was the one time when I'm sure they were convinced that I was being led astray. After a short time, of course, my head recovered its former glory, to my mother's great delight, if not to mine.

49

A few more names come to mind at this point, but again I'm not sure where some of the people worked. I remember Mr. Coates senior, very well. Who could forget such an imposing figure? His son was also a tall, well-built young man with short, crinkly hair. I can't remember where either of them worked, though I think Mr. Coates senior had some responsibility for the Irish Department. Douglas Coates was a man of many parts; I believe he played cricket for the Bradford Cricket Club, and he was also a fluent speaker of Spanish. I think it was due to the friendship that existed between them that Alan Gostick also became interested in learning the Spanish language. After what I've already said about Alan's influence upon me, I hardly dare mention the fact that it wasn't long before I took up an interest in Spanish and actually went to evening classes for a while. After a few months, however, my interest faded away and all I can remember now of the language is the question "Que es esto?", which I think means "What is that?" Not very much, is it?

Another member of staff whom I've not mentioned previously was Charles Wood. I can't remember what position he held, but my recollection is that he was a manager, but of which department I have now no idea. He used to pass through the Counting House fairly frequently on his way to the Board Room, and one of his trade-marks was that he always, yes ALWAYS, carried in his hand a piece of white paper, perhaps a letter or an order, which we thought was intended to make his visit, whatever its purposes, look twice as important! It might have had some connection with a side-line of his. From time to time he used to arrive in the Counting House with a box which contained a number of packages of Irish butter. Presumably it was part of a consignment which had arrived by Passenger Train and which he proceeded to distribute to various members of the senior staff.

I am now almost at the end of MY story. I regret that I haven't a single snapshot or group photograph of anyone who worked at Law, Russell's. The explanation for this inadequacy probably lies in the fact that I cannot recall there being any joint activities in which I was invited to share, such as cricket, football, drama or similar pursuits. I know that some of the staff engaged in various leisure activities, but away from Law, Russell's. It looks as though no-one had considered the advantages for the morale of the employees, of doing some of these things together; it might have helped a little if they had!

50

CHAPTER NINE

Law, Russell House Today

It was a great pity that an old-established firm with such a good reputation in the textile trade, should have had to cease trading. For many of the employees it must have meant the end of their working lives, which in turn, led to those hopeless years on the "dole", because such a large proportion of the workforce was in the forty to fifty age group! For others such as myself, unemployment became a time for learning about the realities, and in its disconcerting way, a preparation for the adventure which is LIFE!

I have the feeling that some people, especially those who are "getting on a bit" and considering setting down some of their recollections of former days, would first of all spend a considerable amount of time in researching the project, so as to avoid the kind of error that can be caused by a lapse of memory.

As Longfellow said "ART IS LONG AND TIME IS FLEETING", so I decided at the age of eighty-two that if I was going to get anything at all written down, I would have to forego a lot of checking and researching, in favour of recording as faithfully as possible as much as I could remember about my life and times, with particular reference to my period of employment in "LITTLE GERMANY". As we all know, the human mind is a wonderful piece of equipment, but it can on occasion, prove to be somewhat fickle. Consequently, if there are mistakes that are obvious to the expert, and which could have been avoided if more time had been spent on checking some of my statements about people or events - then I apologise sincerely!

When I began these memoirs and tried to visualise what the entrance to the Law, Russell building was like just inside the front door, I could only imagine that there were five or six steps up to the ground floor! This may seem to be rather odd, but when I came to read Mr. Roberts' description of the building, I observed that it included the statement that to reach ground level "Meant climbing about eight steps from the entrance since this slight adjustment of floor level meant a radical improvement in the cellar lighting". I realised my mistake then, but to "make assurance double sure," I decided to take a look for myself. My wife and I were in the vicinity so it seemed a good opportunity to visit 63, Vicar Lane - Law, Russell House - and take a look through the front door. I was able to confirm, very quickly, that Mr. Roberts' estimate of the number of steps was much more accurate than mine!

While we were looking through the glass panel of the locked front door, an employee of the Dept. of Social Services came down the steps towards us and, on unlocking the door, enquired if we needed any assistance. I indicated that it would be a great joy for me if we could be permitted just to look around the entrance hall, in order to see what alterations had taken place since I was employed in the office there in 1927! He invited us inside and said that he was a messenger and that his name was Malcolm Mason. I pointed out a few of the obvious changes that had taken place in the entrance hall, such as the re-siting of the passenger lift-shaft, and replacing the old manually driven lift with a quiet-running modern one! The firm's time-clock used to stand against the wall in the position that is now occupied by the stainless steel doors of the lift. The fact that I found it all very exciting must have communicated itself to Mr. Mason for he said that he had a few minutes to spare and would be happy to show us all round the building. This was more than I had dared to hope for; it was like a dream come true! Thank you again, Malcolm!

The internal alterations have changed the premises almost beyond recognition for me. We toured the building from the ground floor right to the top, and it was only later that I realised that we had passed through what was the area of the Counting House, without even realising it as such! A few of the original features are still visible and it was not difficult for me to recognise the area where the well used to be, but the well itself has been enclosed, and the "hole" is no longer to be seen. The white (?) tiled walls of the external well can still be seen, but I do find it difficult, even after touring the building, to think of the building in any other way, (with one or two exceptions) than it used to be!

Once again I must acknowledge the assistance provided by Mr. Roberts' booklet "Little Germany", which probably did more than anything else to get me started on this project; the tour of Law, Russell House was totally unexpected and immensely rewarding!

Finally, for all the encouragement and practical support in obtaining for me a copy of my grandfather's death certificate and also a photocopy of a page of the Bradford Daily Telegraph dated 12th June 1903, which records the result of the inquest into my grandfather's death from drowning, my very warmest thanks and appreciation to my friend Mrs. Mary Twentyman, without whose research and enthusiasm I might have remained unaware of some important details which she uncovered for me. Thanks again, Mary!

So that's my story! It probably doesn't seem to be very much, so I repeat, it is basically the story of about four years only - the formative years of my working life - as an office-boy and clerk in "LITTLE GERMANY", It is the story of my early experiences only, set against a backcloth of the area and the times in which I grew up.

When I had written the previous paragraph I really thought that this was the end of my story. Not surprisingly however, I was left with a question to which I was quite unable to supply an answer; the question, which incidentally was "How and where does the story of the Bradford Trade and its part in the development of Little Germany begin?"

Part Two, therefore, is my inexpert, and no doubt sometimes inaccurate attempt, to supply an answer; not a complete answer, by any means, but a part of the answer. I trust that the following pages will help to stimulate still further the interest of readers in the whole story of an important part of our heritage as citizens of the City of Bradford-

Towards Little Germany

Towards Little Germany

PART TWO

BACK TO THE BEGINNING

(A brief look at how it all began)

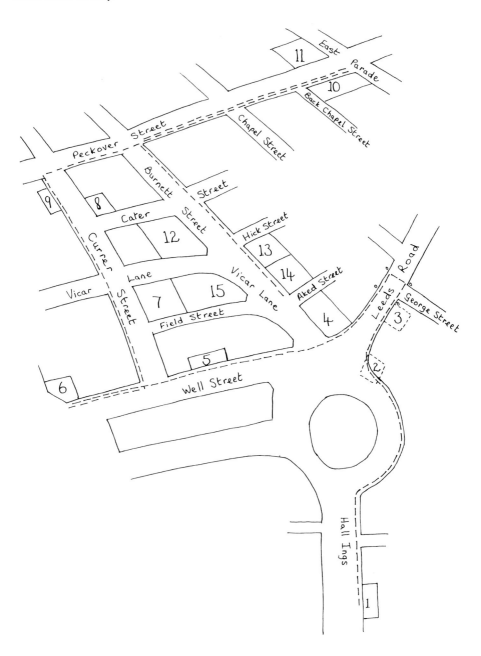

Towards Little Germany

The "Mini-Trail"

1.	*Milligan, Forbes & Co.	Hall Ings	Ch. 10
2.	A. & S. Henry & Co., Ltd.	Leeds Road	Ch. 11
3.	Schuster, Fulda & Co.	62 Leeds Road	Ch. 12
4.	Leigh Mills Co., Ltd.	53-55 Leeds Road	Ch. 12
5.	Stavert, Zigomala & Co.	51-53 Well Street	Ch. 12
6.	*Bradford Dyers' Ass. Ltd.	39 Well Street	Ch. 12
7.	*Downs, Coulter & Co., Ltd.	4 Currer Street	Ch. 13
8.	Firth and Marshall Ltd.	8 Currer Street	Ch. 13
9.	*Wm. Berry & Co. Ltd.	Currer House	
		13 Currer Street	Ch. 13
10.	*Heugh, Dunlop & Co.	46 Peckover Street	Ch. 13
11.	*D. Delius & Co.	Caspian House	
		61 East Parade	Ch. 13
12.	Priestley's Ltd.	66 Vicar Lane	Ch. 13
13.	J. P. Kessler & Co.	64 Vicar Lane	Ch. 13
14.	Devere House	62 Vicar Lane	Ch. 13
15.	*Law, Russell & Co., Ltd.	63 Vicar Lane	Ch. 14

*photographs of these premises appear at the back of the book

57

If you intend to walk this mini-trail
you may wish to obtain a copy of
Stanley Varo's booklet "A Mercantile Meander"
or Bradford Council's free publication
"Bradford's Merchant Trail"
These give architectural information
not covered in this book.

Both these booklets can be obtained from
Bradford Tourist Information Office

CHAPTER TEN

How It All Began

When I had reached this point in my memoirs my appetite had been whetted for learning more about how the Bradford Home Trade began to expand early in the nineteenth century, and how it developed in and around the area which came to be known as Little Germany. This meant of course, that any references to the revolution that was about to take place in the market place would, of necessity, be expressed in a more impersonal manner, that is to say that this part of my story would be concerned much more with the experiences of other people - many other people - rather than my own!

In my limited research into the origins of the Bradford Home Trade Warehouse I found it quite impossible to avoid (even if I wanted to) the name of Milligan, Forbes & Co., in spite of the fact that this firm never occupied premises in Little Germany.

> *(1) We start our mini-trail in Hall Ings, outside what is now the Telegraph and Argus building.*

Milligan, Forbes & Co., was one of the very first firms in Bradford to concentrate entirely on the successful merchanting of textiles. There were, of course, others with the same sort of aims in the first few years of that important decade, but few, if any, whose interest was entirely in textiles! For this reason I am going to let the experience of a young Scot who came to Yorkshire seeking his fortune, serve as my example of how things began.

In the early days of the nineteenth century, actually in the year 1802, Robert Milligan left his home on the family farm in Scotland; a young man with a burning desire to seek his fortune as a "travelling salesman", so first of all he went to join his brother who had already set up a drapery business near Skipton, in Yorkshire.

As a travelling salesman, Robert Milligan carried in a wooden box upon his back what was virtually the contents of a small drapery shop, like a door-to-door salesman in fact, except that the doors were so far apart! By any standards, it was a physically demanding exercise which must have required the utmost dedication to the undertaking, but nevertheless he was eventually able to open a small shop himself in

Westgate, Bradford. After some time he moved to larger premises next to the Talbot Hotel in Kirkgate.

There is little doubt that in addition to his ability as a salesman, Robert Milligan was a shrewd buyer of woollens and linens and it was as a buyer of such merchandise that he was brought into contract with Henry Forbes who was associated with Leo Schuster, one of the first German immigrants to operate in the textile field in this country.

The retail side of Milligan's business was moved from Kirkgate to Piccadilly, and shortly afterwards the home trade house of Milligan, Forbes was born. This was in January 1831. It looks as though the Bradford home trade warehouse evolved quite naturally from the linen drapers' shops which were promoted by various members of the Milligan family, and each Home Trade merchant, because of his skill both as buyer and seller of textile fabrics, was able to keep abreast of public fashions. As a result of such enterprise the Bradford home trade warehouse stocked a range of products, even from the earliest days, which was greater than that which was produced in the Bradford area alone!

This became an important factor in making Bradford a world textile centre, and the company was now operating not only as retail drapers but as wholesalers as well. It almost appears as though some of the problems which had to be met by the manufacturers in the area were simply to be overcome by merchants of the calibre of Milligan, Forbes & Co. For example, if a manufacturer was unable to dispose of all his stock to visiting merchants on Thursday - Market Day, the alternative was for him to take his goods to either Leeds or Manchester. This was an expensive exercise as well as being a time-consuming operation. Consequently the advantages of having a merchant actually established in Bradford was profitable to the sellers and these circumstances gave first choice to Milligan, Forbes & Co., of those goods which were in great demand.

As one looks at the growth of the textile trade, it becomes apparent that the prosperity of the Merchant was closely linked to that of the Dyer and Finisher. Close relationships were formed in other directions too. When Robert Milligan's niece and adopted daughter married H.W. Ripley of Bowling, the link between these two branches of the textile trade was firmly established! On the one hand there was what was probably the most important mercantile firm in Bradford, and on the other what was to become the largest dyeworks in the world! Prosperity for the foreseeable future was bright indeed!

In the year 1853, Milligan, Forbes' new home trade warehouse was built on the water meadows, close to the Bradford Beck, at the bottom of Leeds Road. It has been described as *"One of the earliest warehouse buildings in Bradford, and one of the most attractive, which sets the pattern for warehouse building in the period 1853 - 1873".*

In the climate in which the building of commercial premises had been taking place, (towards the end of the eighteenth century and well into the nineteenth), it was, apparently, not considered to be of any importance that buildings, which were intended for trade and commerce, should possess any aesthetic appeal! Such features as grace and elegance were, of course, quite attractive when seen on public buildings or on the mansions of the aristocracy; but the warehouses of Bradford were, after all, work places and markets, and many of them were situated in the most unpleasant conditions imaginable. Steaming filth flowed by way of muddy yards and alleys and the unculverted beck; towards the equally filthy cesspool that was the canal basin! Consequently, there had seemed to be little profit in designing warehouse buildings that were attractive in appearance. It seems that warehouse design in Bradford had yet to influence local architects and builders, as well as the buyers and sellers of the products of a rapidly growing number of woollen mills.

One wonders what the merchants of Bradford thought about this new concept of warehouse architecture, as the new building, with its clean, classical lines, began to take shape. It was certainly a brave step forward as it replaced the "raw uncouthness" of such premises as the Old Market Hall (1783) which, although it was probably still standing fifty years later, existing drawings suggest that the building was designed in a style of architecture that was already out of date by the time it was erected!

This situation was, however, about to change and quite rapidly too! The Milligan, Forbes building, in Hall Ings, where we begin our trail, as well as being one of the first warehouse buildings in Bradford, was also one of the first to be designed with the object of being satisfying to the eye of the beholder. Surely the architecture of this building had its influence on the warehouses that were subsequently erected in increasing numbers in the area of Little Germany. It was a matter of some personal satisfaction to me to learn that this new building was equipped with a pair of oscillating steam engines made by LOW MOOR IRONWORKS!

This attractive building has, for many years, been in the occupation of the Bradford Telegraph and Argus, and as it was erected at the same time as one of the great concert halls of the country , its position between St. George's' Hall and the former Court House brought a much-needed elegance to that part of Hall Ings!

It is clear that the firm of Milligan, Forbes & Co., played a very important role in bringing prosperity to the town, and even though the premises are just outside the area of Little Germany, they made a significant contribution to the standard of architecture which was followed throughout the whole precinct.

Although it is some years since the Court House was demolished, its loss allowed the construction of the impressive Press Hall. The two remaining buildings, built at the same time as each other, merit rather more than a glance of appreciation from hurrying pedestrians.

Bradford has an excellent record of honouring the men and women who have done so much to improve the lot of their fellows and it is appropriate to mention, before I leave the subject, that one notable result of the success of the partners Robert Milligan and Henry Forbes, was that they both became Mayors of the town. It is to the great credit of Robert Milligan that he was held in such esteem that he became the first Mayor of Bradford in 1847. Two years later, his partner Henry Forbes was also honoured by being made Mayor!

Another well-known industrialist, whose name is synonymous with public service - Titus Salt - was likewise honoured by a grateful community, and he became Bradford's second Mayor, serving between Milligan and Forbes! It was a fine tribute to all three men that their public service was recognised by the people of Bradford.

It cannot have passed unnoticed that Bradford's first three mayors were all Non-Conformists and belonged to the same chapel - Horton Lane Congregational Chapel!

CHAPTER ELEVEN

A Mini-trail Unwinds

(2) We now leave Hall Ings and walk towards the Eastbrook Well roundabout to move along Leeds Road, passing the former sites of the Exchange Railway Station and Peel Place. The grassed area to the right was the site of A. and S. Henry & Co. Ltd. Though not yet in Little Germany, we are getting closer and only a few yards away from what, according to the experts, is its southern boundary!

I am reminded that during the four years that I worked in the area, I passed this spot quite regularly, and certainly twice each day. Henry's headquarters were in Manchester and their original Bradford warehouse was in the Bolton Road part of the town, but as business increased quite dramatically towards the middle of the nineteenth century, they were compelled to look for more commodious premises and ended by having to build their own in Leeds Road. The new building occupied the whole of the south side of Peel Place, between the Exchange Station and Vicar Lane.

There must have been a great deal of building activity taking place in Victorian Bradford during the years between 1850 and 1880, but at the time when warehouses which possessed features of aesthetic merit were only just beginning to be built, Henry's new building was of special interest and it was described as "One of the finest buildings of its kind in the kingdom, being vast in extent and of considerable architectural interest." For more than a hundred years it occupied this prominent position in Leeds Road; almost but not quite in Little Germany, yet having its share of influence on both the trade and the architecture of the area!

Despite the fact that the building was scheduled as being of architectural or historical interest however, by the 1960s the end was in sight and permission was given for it to be demolished. Many people of my generation will remember this find old building with something approaching affection!

I have not come across any record as to how many people were employed by Henry's (perhaps I didn't look hard enough or in the right places), but perhaps the number would be around one hundred to a hundred and fifty, but it seems rather odd to me that, when they had obviously had such a large staff, that I should only be able to remember the name of one person who worked for them in Leeds Road during the 1926-1930 period, and that was a man by the name of John Bryden. I cannot remember what his job was, probably something of a clerical nature such as a stock records clerk. He was the father of two boys who were friends of mine. My father knew him very well, as they were both trustees of the Primitive Methodist Chapel in School Street, Low Moor.

A & S Henry's were involved in "The Bradford Trade". It may seem superfluous to use this description, but what it really means is that they were "Stuff Merchants", who handled a whole range of textile fabrics in the piece, and particularly the worsted fabrics which had largely superseded the heavier woollen cloths in the Bradford area. The worsted materials were generally lighter in weight and smarter in appearance when used for making women's skirts or men's suitings. Henry's played a large part in popularising this type of clothing material, and so the demand thus created for a better class of wool fabric was an advantage to the local manufacturers, who were in competition with the French manufacturers, since they (the French) had achieved a certain reputation in the production of good quality all-wool fabrics!

In my search for information concerning the origins of some of the merchanting houses of Little Germany, I found that the name of Leo Schuster kept appearing, just as I had found earlier in the case of Robert Milligan, though perhaps not quite to the same extent. For me, this meant that the name was important and that the owner's contribution to the textile trade was probably considerable, and of particular interest as I continued to trace the growth of the worsted industry in Bradford.

Not altogether surprisingly, I discovered that the two men, Milligan and Schuster, had been associated in business together in Manchester and that Robert Milligan was employed for a period as buyer for Leo Schuster;   this was in the year 1825, or thereabouts.

It was about this time that a woolcombers' strike for more wages, a strike which lasted for twenty-three weeks, caused a great deal of hardship amongst the workpeople and their families, if not quite so much amongst their employers! When this strike was followed, after a few months, by a series of riots which occurred as a result of the introduction of power loom weaving, the future for the industry was looking black indeed!   In fact, in the face of all the obstacles, and in spite of the severe difficulties experienced by the workers, the industry was undoubtedly expanding. There were several factors involved in this state of affairs. Perhaps the principal contribution to the improving situation was the introduction of cotton warps in the manufacture of worsted material, and as Joseph Fieldhouse pointed out in his book "BRADFORD" :-

"Power loom weaving placed a great strain on the threads, and cotton, being stronger and cheaper than wool was found to be an excellent substitute."

and James Parker, in his book "30 Villages from Hipperholme to Tong" seems to support this view!

Incidentally, I have in my possession a copy of this book which was given to my father by the late Alderman William Warburton, and the book is one which I found to be of increasing interest to me as the years have gone by!

In addition to the use of cotton warps, there were, of course, other factors involved in ensuring a growing textile trade. For example, more and more machinery was being designed to aid the spinning and weaving processes, so that the expansion of the worsted industry in particular was progressing rapidly. Wool combing was still mainly done by hand, since no machinery had been invented at this time which could perform the combing operation to the same high standard as hand combing; but another factor was also advantageous to Bradford's wool textile manufacturers! Formerly most of the wool cloth which was woven in Bradford was brought by merchants from Leeds in the "grey" state, and after the dyeing and finishing process had been carried out, the materials were frequently exported to Germany, America and other places abroad! Happily for the prosperity of the Bradford merchants, this situation was about to change!

As the local dyeing and finishing industry was also making quite remarkable progress, this ensured that the local engineering firms were enabled to seize their share of the opportunities that were offered by the textile industry, and they were encouraged to design and manufacture newer and yet more efficient machinery, so that altogether the prosperity of Bradford seemed to be assured! In this regard, John James wrote :-

> Among all the improvements in machinery none excels that of the Jacquard Loom, by which the most beautiful and complicated patterns are embroidered upon, and woven in the piece.

In the first part of this book, when I was writing about the members of the Counting House staff at Law, Russell's, I mentioned the name of Mrs. Lina Walker, and I said that the name "LINA" was a name that I had not heard before. I remembered this when I was reading John James on the subject of patterned worsteds, in which connection he quoted the following lines, attributed to Darwin :-

> "Inventress of the woof, fair "LINA" flings
> The flying shuttle thro' the dancing strings,

Inlays the broidered weft with flowery dyes;
Quick beat the reeds, the pedals fall and rise :
Now from the beam the lengths of warp unwind;
And dance and nod the massy weights behind"

This use of the name "LINA" I found interesting, especially since in some way it was connected with the worsted industry, though I have not yet discovered what the connection was. Perhaps I shall discover who the lady was, before I have finished this book ! *

It must be obvious to anyone remotely connected with the industry that I know very little about the subject of cloth manufacture! After reading the lines attributed to Darwin I was reminded of much of the atmosphere of the weaving shed that I remember from my boyhood!

My mother's youngest sister was a weaver, and sometimes I was permitted to accompany my mother when she went to speak to my Aunt when she was working at the loom. What I remember most was not only the flying shuttle or the "clack-clack" of the "picking stick" as it sent the shuttle rapidly back and forth across the frame, but more than anything else it was the volume of noise, generally - quite frightening to a young child. The weavers, I remember, used a kind of silent sign language; I recall that I found that conversation with my mother and my aunt was quite impossible!

I regret to say that my enquiries have not revealed the lady's name.

CHAPTER TWELVE

Acorns And Oaks

(3) Continue on the same side of Leeds Road to view the former site of Schuster, Fulda & Co. before coming to George Street

I now return to the period between the years 1820 and 1830, for it was during this period of change and opportunity that immigrant traders from the continent began to arrive in Bradford. Generally speaking, trade was dominated by local people, but the very first foreign merchant to build his own premises in Bradford was Leo Schuster, and this fact alone makes his contribution to the Bradford textile scene very important indeed.

By 1829 he had founded the firm of Schuster, Fulda & Co., occupying small premises on Union Street, on the site where the Norfolk Gardens Hotel is now situated, and then in 1826 the firm went on to purchase the site in Leeds Road, at the end of George Street, immediately opposite where Eastbrook Hall was to be built in 1903. This Christian edifice IS in Little Germany, but how long it will remain I hesitate to forecast. It closed in 1986 and has remained empty ever since and was damaged by a serious fire in February 1996.

The firm of Schuster, Fulda is long gone, like many of the firms who did so much to enrich Bradford's reputation as a merchanting centre, with little save the written word in many cases, to mark the passing of what was once a flourishing business of world-wide reputation.

(4) Cross Leeds Road at the traffic lights by Eastbrook Hall. Turn left and on the right hand corner of Vicar Lane are the premises where the Bradford warehouse of the Leigh Mills Co. Ltd., was located.

(5) Walk along Well Street, past Kershaw House. Austral House is now numbered 51 and 53 Well Street.

I remember the part of the building that was numbered 53, Well Street, but who occupied the remainder of the building I have now no recollection.

I was born in 1910, so that by the time that the First World War occurred, I was just beginning to take notice of scraps of conversation that passed between my mother and father. Sometimes these little bits of information were not intended for my ears! Some of those scraps of conversation, although not meaning very much to me at the time, in some quite inexplicable way have stayed in the recess of my mind for well over three-quarters of a century! One such snippet had to do with my father's occupation before I was born, though I am not exactly sure when it would have been. I do remember though, quite vividly, my father saying to my mother on more than one occasion - "When I worked at Stafford, Zigomalar's ... etc." - at least, that is what it sounded like to me! Of course, it meant nothing at all at the time and that was all I knew until quite recently!

I was searching around for more facts about Little Germany, (the boffins probably call it "researching") and I was looking through a book that I had borrowed from the Wibsey Library, when I found an item that was of particular interest to me, and which brought certain things into focus. I was quite elated with my discovery. The book was called "Victorian Bradford - The Living Past", an excellent book introduced by David James with some striking photographs by Ian Beesley.

There seems to be little doubt that the first name in the company's title was not "Stafford" but "Stavert", perhaps a German name. The second name, however, is given by David James as "Zigmata", which is not as I remember the name when used by my father. There is no doubt at all in my mind that the name was not "Zigmata" but "Zignomala", with the syllables spoken very quickly and with the accent on the last syllable, to rhyme with "Ma" or "Pa"! This is how the name is spelt on Goad's map of the area around Law, Russell's!

Stavert, Zigomala & Co., who were stuff merchants, were just another of those firms who did so much to make Little Germany important, both as a merchanting centre and as an example of fine Victorian architecture! Their premises - Austral House in Well Street - may not have been all that could have been desired internally, but externally it is still one of the most attractive buildings with many decorative features which are worthy of a long look of appreciation. Admittedly, many of these old buildings possess attractive characteristics which are often unobserved by the man-in-the-street, and I confess that, prior to starting work on this project, I was just such a man-in-the-street! But no more! I am at last beginning to augment my appreciation of the Victorian warehouse in a manner that I never knew previously, except for the special kind of interest that I had taken in my former workplace - Law, Russell House!

I do not know at what age I began to take some notice of the large warehouse and office buildings in the centre of Bradford. I couldn't have been very old, perhaps five or six years of age when I began to notice that some buildings were different from others, and that in some way, some buildings were much nicer to look at than others. I don't think that this was something that I had very strong feelings about, but I probably possessed the germ of an interest in the work of the stone-mason, as my grandfather and an uncle were both stone-masons. I am sure that at quite an early age, despite the fact that the grandfather referred to had died before I was born, I would be picking up the occasional reference by members of the family, to the work of the stone-mason.

(6) Continue to Pennine House, the premises of Pulse Radio, at the junction of Well Street and Church Bank.

Amongst the buildings that early on in life I recognised as being rather special, was the extensive B.D.A. (Bradford Dyers' Association) building at the bottom of Church Bank, on the corner of Well Street. It was a massive block of premises, as it still is of course, but I knew then, that it was "Special" - well, my Dad worked there, didn't he? That was sufficient to make the building at 39, Well Street, "special"!

I remember clearly an occasion when I was quite small, being taken by my mother up Church Bank, and standing in the grounds of the Parish Church (where my paternal grandparents were married!), and waving excitedly to my father who was waving back to us from a window on the third or fourth floor of the B.D.A. building where he worked as a stuff warehouseman. I remember that he came down to the front door to talk to us. What the conversation was about, I can only guess, but as my mother seldom went into the centre of Bradford unless accompanied by another adult, it seems likely that she had been taking me to keep a dental appointment at the school clinic in Manor Row; and was reporting to my father on the outcome. If that is what she was doing, I cannot recall if it was anything more than a routine examination.

In those early years, the letters B.D.A. were to me three of the most important letters in the alphabet and I felt sure that the firm was the most important in the whole world! It is not surprising therefore, that I grew up in the belief that the B.D.A. building was a "special" building!

A gentleman by the name of David Everett, who lived at the end of the eighteenth century and a little way into the nineteenth, might have been thinking about the "Bradford Trade", although I am quite sure that he wasn't, when he wrote the following lines :-
"Large streams from little fountains flow,

69

Tall oaks from little acorns grow"

I believe that the reasoning behind those words was never more clearly demonstrated than when used, as I use them now, in connection with Little Germany and the Bradford trade! As the title indicates The Bradford Dyers' Association Ltd., was an association of companies whose business was the dyeing trade, who came together to support each other to their mutual advantage. While many names instantly spring to mind, such as Sharp's Low Moor, Hunsworth Dyeing Co., Wm. Grandage & Co., and others, all names that I used to hear frequently in conversation within the family. There is no doubt in my mind though, that the principal member of the association was Edwd. Ripley & Sons Ltd, of Bowling Dyeworks.

At the beginning of the present century it was not only the oldest dyeing company in the association, but it was also the largest; in fact it was reported to be the largest dyeworks in the world! Like so many other vast business empires it started in a very small way, and the first dyehouse operated by the Ripley family was a very small affair indeed, as can be judged from an illustration in James Parker's "Illustrated History", which, as matter of interest, is dedicated to Mr. James Sharp F.C.S., Shirley Manor, WIKE, who retired from active involvement in business life when the Bradford Dyers' Association was formed.

As a small boy, if there was one company's name that I used to hear more than any other, apart from that of the B.D.A. itself, it was that of Ripleys - Edward Ripley & Son, of Bowling Dyeworks. For a long time I am sure that I thought that the name "Ripley's" was synonymous with that of the B.D.A.. I know that I used to hear the names of several other dyeing companies mentioned, but Ripley's was the important one! So if, in the course of this account it seems that I am writing about Ripley's, that's how it was for me. The B.D.A. was mainly Ripley's of Bowling Dyeworks - the others I didn't know very much about, and in my ignorance I didn't believe that they could possibly count for very much! Even though Ripley's Dyeworks were part of the history of Bowling and not Little Germany, I feel that I cannot tell my story about the B.D.A., however briefly, without it sounding a bit like the story of Ripley's of Bowling Dyeworks.

The dyeing industry was established in Bowling very early in the nineteenth century, on a site which had at one time been occupied by three cottages, so it was a very modest venture in the beginning. James Parker tells us that a Mr. Walton held the tenancy of a little dyehouse in 1804, but by 1812 George Ripley, who was a practical dyer, having learnt his trade in Halifax, joined Walton at Bowling and together they developed the activities of the little dyeworks. There was already distinct signs of growth when George Ripley's son Edward, who had also learnt the dyeing business, was taken into partnership and by 1822 the firm had adopted its new title of George Ripley & Sons, Dyers.

Mrs. Anne Ripley, the wife of Edward, was sufficiently interested in the success of her husband's enterprise, that she involved herself in assisting in the promotion of the business, and a room was taken in the Old Talbot Inn yard, in Hustlergate, where she attended on Mondays and Thursdays. As an example of her industry, Parker records that "Nearly a cart-load of goods were sent from the Talbot Inn room to Bowling Dyeworks, every week!"

For many years Ripley's Bowling Dyeworks were successfully operated, and held a commanding position in the textile trade, as did the Association of which it was a major part. Unfortunately, in common with many other groups, large and small, during the past twenty years or so, they too were victims of a world-wide recession in the trade; and today, the sign that used to look down over Forster Square, announcing in letters of gold, (?) that these were the premises of "The Bradford Dyers' Association Ltd.," have been removed and the whole block, with its display of "TO LET" signs, no longer reflects its former glory!

CHAPTER THIRTEEN

Different Buildings

(7) We now retrace our steps and go back along Well Street, turning left up Currer Street, to look at several of the buildings which I knew so well long ago! The doorway at the corner of Field Street marks the premises which were formerly occupied by Downs Coulter & Co., Ltd., for many years a thriving company manufacturing linings in their own mills at Pudsey.

The firm began trading in 1893, and I believe that it was in 1917 that they moved to the warehouse premises in Currer Street. They also had their own cotton mill in Lancashire and had been successful in opening up a promising shipping trade. In the latter part of 1976 however, the firm transferred its warehouse to Thornton Mills, and vacated this once-impressive building.

During the past couple of years, on my visits to the area (which I confess, have become fewer and fewer with the passing years) I have witnessed the former Downs, Coulter warehouse standing there like a skeleton following the disastrous fire which occurred a few years ago. Until fairly recently the shell of the building was allowed to remain, apparently untouched, looking sad and neglected.

Now, however (1997) the building is, happily, being restored again in spite of the vandalism which has interfered with progress. The huge listed warehouse will eventually provide bed-sitters for single, young and homeless people, and also provide 38 much-needed flats, close to the facilities offered by Little Germany.

(8) Continuing up Currer Street, at number 8 on the corner of Cater Street was the firm of Firth & Marshall Ltd.

I cannot recall that I knew much about this firm's activities, but I believe they were Stuff Merchants, as so many firms in the area were. I did know one man who worked for them - Harry Scott from Wyke, a local baritone singer of repute. I believe it was also to Firth and Marshall that Herbert Bearpark went when LR's was about to close.

(9) On the opposite side of the street, at number 13, was the building that used to be occupied by William Berry & Co., Ltd.. now called Currer House.

I have already mentioned in Part I that during the late 20's when trading conditions were becoming extremely difficult for many Bradford merchanting warehouses, the firm of William Berry & Co. Ltd. was incorporated with Law, Russell's and as a result they left their premises in Currer Street, bringing with them most of their staff. Sadly, it seems that by that time, there was very little hope of saving either them or Law, Russell's!

We now walk to the top of Currer Street and turn right into Peckover Street.

There are some interesting buildings here that I knew long ago, without actually knowing anything about the occupants of the buildings, or the trade that they carried on in the 1920s. Some of these merchanting houses were started by German immigrants who, to their credit, played an active part in building up the "Bradford Trade", as well as being to the forefront in public service as patrons of the arts, especially music!

Some of them were stuff merchants, while others operated mainly as yarn merchants; one such firm was A. Hoffman & Co., whose warehouse was at 8 Burnett Street. As a prominent member of the Chamber of Commerce, Achior Hoffman worked tirelessly to promote the desirability of Bradford possessing a Wool Conditioning House, stressing the advantages and benefits to the trade such laboratory controls would bring. It was due in large measure to his energy and powers of persuasion, that his idea became a reality. Naturally, without receiving plenty of support he would not have been successful, but in 1891 the Bradford Conditioning House was opened!

(10) Continue to 46, Peckover Street at the junction with East Parade.

As a young lad working in the area, I was always impressed by this building. The premises were built for the firm of Heugh, Dunlop & Co., home trade merchants and the partners, both Scots, were John Heugh, who lived in Manchester, and Walter Dunlop from Bingley, Yorkshire.

To my inexpert eyes I knew that in some way, this building was different from most of the other warehouses round about, though I would have found it difficult at the time, to say why! The premises were designed by a leading Leeds architect named George Corson, which may be some indication why the building looked different and unlike any of the other warehouses built in what I can only call "The Bradford Warehouse Style"! It seems likely to me that the building had more affinity with the Leeds warehouses of that period!

(11) Opposite number 46 is 61, East Parade known as Caspian House.

In addition to being stuff merchants, a few firms managed to operate as yarn merchants and shippers, as well! The firm of D. Delius & Co., (another firm of German origin) were in this category, and they operated from the premises at 61, East Parade, now known as Caspian House. Perhaps our chief interest in the firm today lies in the fact that Julius Delius, who was the senior partner in the firm, was the father of the famous composer Frederick Delius!

We are nearing the end of our "Mini-Trail", and now we take a look at the premises of a couple of Law, Russell's nearest neighbours.

(12) Retrace our steps back along Peckover Street and turn down Burnett Street. We come to the premises of Priestleys Ltd., 66, Vicar Lane, opposite Hick Street at the corner where Burnett Street ends, and Vicar Lane sweeps away in the direction of Currer Street and Church Bank. (At the time of this book's preparation in early 1997 the building was reduced to a shell and surrounded by scaffolding.)

Priestley's building is another of Little Germany's classical buildings. Although not as large and imposing as the Law, Russell building nevertheless, it still retains its own brand of elegance and charm, in an area where these qualities are to be found in abundance!

The premises were acquired by Briggs Priestley & Sons, who were, I believe, manufacturers of dress materials. In 1901 the name of the company was changed to Priestleys Ltd., and like many other manufacturers at that time, saw the advantages to be gained by merchanting their own materials; and, in so doing, established a world wide reputation as suppliers of the best in dress materials! Their accomplishments in this direction also did a great deal toward the success of the dyeing and finishing industry in Bradford, for it was reported that the products of Priestley's looms were ALL sent to Bowling Dyeworks to be dyed and finished, and consequently, in making their contribution to Ripley's world-wide reputation, Priestleys did much to enhance the cause of the Bradford trade! Unfortunately, Priestley's premises too, have been unoccupied for a long time and are awaiting new tenants!

(13) & (14) We move to look at the buildings at 64 Vicar Lane and Devere House number 62 .

Even a "Mini-trail" of Little Germany would be incomplete without some reference to the firm of Kesslers' and the premises at 64, Vicar Lane. During the years when I was working in Little Germany, it was hardly possible for me to enter Law, Russell's by the front door, without being aware of the pair of buildings straight opposite. Kesslers' at No. 64 was the upper of the two; as regards the lower building to which it was attached - Devere House, 62, Vicar Lane, at the corner of Aked Street, I have no recollection whatever who the occupants were! Whilst I had a nodding acquaintance with one or two of the lads who worked at Kesslers', I have no such recollection of anyone who worked at No. 62!

Kesslers' was started by a German family who came from Frankfurt and who, in about the year 1830, established a warehouse in Manchester for the purpose of exporting textiles to Germany. After they became the occupants of the warehouse in Vicar Lane, they began to concentrate on trade with America, and as a consequence of broadening their operations, they opened up a wool merchanting department and in 1909 became one of the very first firms to be involved in the export of tops and noils!

CHAPTER FOURTEEN

The End Of The Trail

I end this brief account of the activities of a few of those firms whose buildings I was more familiar with a long time ago, by referring to the one which was the most important of all to me - Law, Russell & Co. Ltd., straight across from Kesslers'.

(15) Look across the road to view the building at 63. Vicar Lane.

John Russell and John Douglas were both drapers when, in 1837, they founded the home trade house of Russell, Douglas & Co., and later occupied the former premises of Robert Milligan in Kirkgate and in Piccadilly. No doubt it was as a result of increasing business that they needed to move their warehouse again after a while, this time near to the bottom of Leeds Road, to premises they named "Russell Buildings", near to the site where Bowling Beck flowed under Cuckoo Bridge, and where Britannia House was later erected, following the re-channelling of the Beck.

In 1842 James Law joined the firm as Bookkeeper and it seems that as a direct result of his diligence, he became senior partner in the company, and the name was changed to Law, Russell & Co. By 1874 the firm had moved to their prominent new premises in Vicar Lane, which were completed for them in a matter of nineteen months! The architects were Lockwood and Mawson, one of the leaders of their profession in Bradford, if not THE leaders! They were the architects responsible for the design of such prestigious buildings as the Town Hall, the Wool Exchange and St. George's Hall! The contractor for the Law, Russell building (as well as several other buildings in Little Germany) was Archibald Neil. He was very much before his time in that he was a pioneer of improved building techniques, and also a model employer in his relationships with those who worked for him. There were frequently as many as fourteen hundred employed by him at any one time - in his quarries, brickworks and carpenters' shops.

Mention of Britannia House above, brings back memories of seeing this site being excavated in preparation for the new building, and my recollection of that part of the Central Area Development Scheme is that of a huge digging operation which involved the use of heavy pile-drivers that were necessary to enable the foundations to be laid on a sound base. One of the problems, perhaps the greatest problem, was that of controlling the flow of water on such a vulnerable site, which was a veritable confluence of underground streams, notably those of the Bradford Beck and Bowling Beck. I am firmly of the opinion, from my observations at the time, that it was a terrific struggle to keep the workings free of water, and I recall that large pumps were constantly at work to this end!

And finally, to repeat my admiration of the premises at 63, Vicar Lane, I should say that, in common with other neighbouring warehouses, it clearly seems to have been built with the aim of being pleasing to look at with its sometimes extravagant architecture, by today's standards(?) on the one hand, and being attractive to customers with its well-designed interior, on the other! One can close by saying, with little fear of contradiction, that Little Germany is a fine example of the highly successful association of the combined abilities of Victorian Bradford's Architects, Builders and Merchants. May we never lose the will to preserve, for future generations, our Heritage -

Details of Photographs on the following pages:-

P79   **Photograph of the author, Mr Norman Ellis,** taken in 1927.
© N. Ellis

P80   **Mini-Trail item 1 - Chapter 10**
Milligan, Forbes & Co warehouse in Hall Ings, now the "Telegraph
and Argus" building, from "The Warehouseman and Draper" 1899 .
© Bradford Industrial Museum. We are grateful to Mr Ian Ward
of the Museum for tracking down this photograph.

P81   **Mini-Trail item 6 - Chapter 12**
Bradford Dyers' Association Ltd., 39 Well Street, now Pennine House. We
are grateful to Mrs Dorothy Burrows, the copyright holder, who supplied us
with this photograph which was probably taken in the 1950's.

P82   **Mini-Trail item 7 - Chapter 13**
Downs Coulter & Co. Ltd., 4 Currer Street taken in 1996.

P83   **Mini-Trail item 9 - Chapter 13**
Wm. Berry & Co. Ltd., Currer House, 13 Currer Street - 1996

P84   **Mini-Trail item 10 - Chapter 13**
Heugh, Dunlop & Co. 46 Peckover Street - 1996

P85   **Mini-Trail item 11 - Chapter 13**
D. Delius & Co., Caspian House, 61 East Parade - 1996

P86   **Mini-Trail item 15 - Chapter 14**
Law, Russell & Co. Ltd., 63 Vicar Lane

P87   **The author, Norman Ellis,** taken in 1997.

Unless stated otherwise photographs are copyright © Eric Slicer.

The author, Mr Norman Ellis, taken in 1927.

Towards Little Germany

Mini-Trail item 1 - Chapter 10
Milligan, Forbes & Co warehouse in Hall Ings

Mini-Trail item 6 - Chapter 12
Bradford Dyers' Association Ltd., 39 Well Street, now Pennine House.

Mini-Trail item 7 - Chapter 13
Downs Coulter & Co. Ltd., 4 Currer Street taken in 1996.

Mini-Trail item 9 - Chapter 13
Wm. Berry & Co. Ltd., Currer House, 13 Currer Street - 1996

Mini-Trail item 10 - Chapter 13
Heugh, Dunlop & Co. 46 Peckover Street - 1996

Mini-Trail item 11 - Chapter 13
D. Delius & Co., Caspian House, 61 East Parade - 1996

Mini-Trail item 14 - Chapter 13
Devere House, 62 Vicar Lane - right of photograph.
Mini-Trail item 15 - Chapter 14
Law, Russell & Co. Ltd., 63 Vicar Lane - left of photograph

The author, Norman Ellis, taken in 1997.

LIST OF ALL THE EMPLOYEES WHO WORKED FOR LAW, RUSSELL & CO LTD

During the years 1927 to 1930, whose names I still remember

Adams, Bill	*Counting House*	**Hitt, A. Lloyd**	*Fancy Room*
Ainsworth, Kenneth	*Counting House*	**Hitt, Arthur,**	*Managing Director*
Batchelor, Charles	*Director - Plain Department*	**Hodgkinson, Joe**	*Shipping Department*
Baxter, Bill	*Pattern Room*	**Hodgkinson, Percy**	*Entering Department*
Beard, Leslie	*Fancy Room*	**Hodgson, Miss F.**	*Telephone Switchboard*
Bearpark, Herbert	*Plain Department.*	**Hopkinson, Raymond**	*Top Room*
Berry, William	*Director - Linings Department*	**Jagger, Arnold**	*Counting House*
Bottomley, Miss J.	*Fancy Room*	**Jason-Wood, Miss D.**	*Secretary to Belgian Consul*
Boulton, Dick	*Caretaker etc.*	**Jowett, Maurice**	*Linings Department*
Bradbury, Mr. ?	*Manager - Blanket Department*	**Law, James D.**	*Director and Belgian Consul*
Brady, Miss J.	*Counting House*	**Law, Kenneth W.**	*Company Secretary - Director*
Brayshaw, Lawrence	*Sales Representative*	**Law, Ralph**	*Director - Shipping Department*
Briggs, Mr ?	*Manager - Grey Room*	**Leach, John W**	*Off Manager*
Brown, Walter	*Plain Department.*	**London, Bottomley**	*Counting House*
Catling, Norman	*Entering Department*	**Luscombe, George**	*Shipping Department*
Catling, Sydney	*Shipping Department*	**Magson, Herbert**	*?*
Catling, Willie	*Manager - London Room*	**Magson, Jim**	*Pattern Room*
Catton, Mr.?	*Umbrella Fabrics*	**Mitchell, Miss D.**	*William Berry and Co Ltd*
Clark, Leonard	*Pattern Room*	**Moore, Herbert**	*Shipping Department*
Clarkson, Willie	*Counting House*	**Parker, Percy**	*Manager - Entering Department*
Coates, Douglas	*?*	**Pawson, Fred**	*Counting House*
Coates, (Senior) Mr.	*Irish Department.*	**Peatfield, Eddie**	*Entering Department*
Collett, Fred	*Blanket Room*	**Pickard, Philip**	*Sales Representative*
Cooke, Mrs.	*Office Cleaner*	**Pickard, (Senior) Mr**	*Sales Representative*
Crossley, Miss M	*Counting House*	**Piercey, Miss D.**	*London Room*
Davison, Harry	*Manager - Warehouse/Packing*	**Punt, Harry**	*Irish Department*
Day, Barak	*Boilerman*	**Rayner, Joe**	*Plain Department*
Dixon, Ronald N	*Counting House*	**Redman, James**	*Commisionaire/ Lift*
Dodgson, Charles	*Counting House*	**Robertshaw, Stanley**	*Counting House*
Ellis, Norman	*Counting House*	**Robertshaw, W.**	*Counting House*
Emmett, Harry	*Counting House*	**Robinson, Harry**	*Grey Room*
Flaherty, John	*Plain Department.*	**Rushton, Stanley**	*Fancy Room*
Fox, Cecil	*Fancy Room*	**Rycroft, Herbert**	*Pattern Room*
Fuller, Leslie	*Warehouse Junior*	**Shepherd, Stanley**	*Warehouse Junior*
Gadd, Walter	*William Berry and Co Ltd*	**Sproat, Dick**	*Entering Department*
Galloway ?	*Packing Room*	**Sugden, George**	*Cashier*
Garnett, Horace,	*Fancy Room*	**Sugden, Norman**	*Counting House*
Gostick, Alan	*Counting House*	**Taylor, W**	*Manager Umbrella Fabrics*
Garnett, Wilfred	*London Room*	**Veal, Raymond**	*Assistant Cashier*
Griffiths, Harry,	*Packing Room*	**Walker, Herbert**	*Maintenance*
Hainsworth, John	*Plain Department*	**Walker, Mrs Lina**	*Counting House*
Hall, Ralph	*Counting House*	**Weston, Mrs**	*Cook*
Hall, Victor	*Plain Department.*	**Wilkinson, Ernest**	*Sales Representative*
Hanson, John	*Plain Department.*	**Wilson, Arthur**	*Pattern Room*
Hardaker, Douglas	*Entering Department*	**Wood, Charles**	*?*
Harrison, Fred	*Entering Department*	**Wood, Lewis**	*Pattern Room*